# THE BOOK OF
# CREDITON

## A Celebration of Kirton and Kirtonians

JOHN HEAL

HALSGROVE

First published in Great Britain in 2004

British Library Cataloguing-in-Publication Data.
A CIP record for this title is available from the British Library.

ISBN 1 84114 331 6

HALSGROVE

Halsgrove House
Lower Moor Way
Tiverton, Devon EX16 6SS
Tel: 01884 243242
Fax: 01884 243325
E-mail: sales@halsgrove.com
Website: www.halsgrove.com

Frontispiece photograph: *High Street looking towards Union Street and 'The Lynch'. Although there appears to be a light dusting of snow on the ground it must be an optical illusion as the pedestrians are wearing summer clothing.*

Printed and bound in Great Britain by CPI Bath

# PREFACE

The idea of writing a book about Crediton grew out of a number of conversations with fellow members of the Crediton Area History and Museum Society. The motto of the Society is 'preserving the past for the present and the present for the future', and the initial idea was to produce a booklet that met that ideal. It was around the same time as these discussions were taking place that I discovered some other publications in the Halsgrove Community History Series and decided to investigate the possibilities of producing a book for Crediton. I felt that a town which could boast such illustrious persons as St Boniface and General Buller should surely be worth celebrating in words and pictures.

This book is very much about the community. During my research and preparation I have had the privilege of speaking with a number of Crediton people, but by no means as many as I would have liked. It has been a real pleasure to meet some of our older citizens and to listen to them reminisce about Crediton past. Hopefully their memories and knowledge can be recorded in full before it is too late. However, that is perhaps a project for the future, but not too far into the future.

This book is not intended to be a serious work of history. It is hoped that, as well as telling the story of Crediton past, it will bring back memories and also amuse. As someone who has lived in the town almost all of his life I feel proud to be a Kirtonian, and also proud to be allowed to produce something that will celebrate this fine town of ours.

**John Heal,**
**2004.**

*Oxford Terrace, Mill Street, decorated for the coronation celebrations in 1953.* (PHOTO AUTHERS)

*East Street, c.1922. The fountain is visible in the background.* (CAHMS, F. HURFORD COLLECTION)

# CONTENTS

| | | |
|---|---|---|
| | *Preface* | 3 |
| | *Acknowledgements* | 7 |
| | *Introduction* | 9 |
| *Chapter 1* | **A Settlement by the Creedy** | 11 |
| *Chapter 2* | **St Boniface: The Greatest Englishman**\* | 15 |
| *Chapter 3* | **The Church of the Holy Cross** | 19 |
| *Chapter 4* | **Catholics and Dissenters in Crediton** | 31 |
| *Chapter 5* | **'Kirton was a Market Town'** | 37 |
| *Chapter 6* | **Notable Families and their Homes** | 59 |
| *Chapter 7* | **Industry Past and Present** | 69 |
| *Chapter 8* | **Fire, Flood and Plague** | 83 |
| *Chapter 9* | **Education in Crediton** | 91 |
| *Chapter 10* | **Inns and Hotels** | 97 |
| *Chapter 11* | **Crediton at Play** | 105 |
| *Chapter 12* | **Transport** | 133 |
| *Chapter 13* | **Crediton in Time of War** | 141 |
| *Chapter 14* | **Some Notable Kirtonians of Modern Times** | 149 |
| | *Bibliography* | 157 |
| | *Subscribers* | 158 |

\*Title taken from Timothy Reuter's book of the same name, published by Paternoster Press, Exeter, 1980.

*A triumphal arch in Charlotte Street with crowds beginning to gather to await the return of General Buller from the Boer War. (CAHMS)*

*April Great Market with cattle pens stretching almost up to the Green. (Mrs W. Davey)*

# Acknowledgements

Many people have contributed towards the making of this book. In particular I must thank the members and executive committee of the Crediton Area History and Museum Society for granting me free access to their archives, in particular to the 'Wednesday team' who have tolerated me concentrating on this project and neglecting my other duties over the past 12 months or so. I would like to give particular thanks to the archivist, John Jones, who has proved a great help in giving me access to the Society's collection of photographs and postcards. I would also like to make special mention of Sue Reed of the *Crediton Country Courier* who has not only allowed me to use a number of photographs from her archives but has spent a great deal of time in her busy life searching for items that I have requested. Back issues of this newspaper have also proved a valuable source of information. Special thanks are also due to Mr Les Berry, son of S.J. Berry, and Mrs Miriam Leach, daughter of Bertram Authers, who have given permission for their parents' photographs to be used. I must also recognise the valuable contribution made towards my research by a number of libraries and other archives, and by the staff who work in them. These are: the Crediton Town Library, the University of Exeter Library, the Devon Record Office, the Westountry Studies Library and the Devon and Exeter Institute. Thanks are also due to the people who have contributed articles or have allowed me to use articles that they have previously written; credit is given in the text where I have used such material.

There are many other people whose help has been invaluable, ranging from those who have lent me a single photograph to those who have allowed me to use their research material. They are listed below alphabetically because to attempt to assess the value of each contribution would be an impossible task. They are: Arthur Arscott, Mrs Arscott, Les Ashplant, Dora Blackmore, Mary Blamey, Frank Bristow, Becky Brooks, Sue Brown, Ann Cann, Helen Cann, Ivor Coram, Win Davey, Alan Discombe, Michael Discombe, Revd Sidney Dixon, Norah Fowles, Michael Fennessy, Colin Fribbens, Glenis Fribbens, Nan Gaskell, Chris Gillard, Joan Grant, Dave Green, Yvonne Green, Charlie Greenslade, Ann Grubb, John Grubb, Ron Hamlin, Paul Harris, Kevin Harvey, Les Haydon, Diane Heggadon, Alec Hill, Henry Hill, Sheila Hill, Janet Hopper, Ron Joslin, Robin Langhorne, A. Lee, Michael Lee, 'Pip' Lee, Simon Lee, Martin Maggs, Peter Mashford, Henry Parker, Angela Perkins, Keith Phillips, Mr Plimsole, Jean Roach, Arthur King Robinson, Margaret Sandercock, Ken Saunders, Tim Sedgwick, Nigel Sercombe, Mark Smith, Phil Smith, Margaret Spry, Alan Stoyle, Carolyn Stoyle, Babs Stutchbury, John Theedom, Peter Tregale, Judy Tucker, Margaret Tucker, Ken Turner, Jo Ward, Colin White, David White, Margaret Wollacott. Hopefully I have not missed anybody, but if I have, I apologise, and offer grateful thanks for their contribution.

Finally I would like to thank my wife Jill for the contribution she has made. She has a good eye for the right photograph to use, and has helped with proofreading. Also, she has tolerated the virtual loss of the use of our dining-room for many months and has put up with papers strewn around the room. But most of all she has been there as a supporter and friend.

*Crediton Sunday schools parade, 1907.*
*(CAHMS PLIMSOLE COLLECTION)*

*Crediton Constabulary bicycle parade, c.1900, in a photo taken at the top of Jockey Hill.*

*(CAHMS)*

*Crediton High Street. Note the early street lights hung over the centre of the road – this dates the photo later than 1929. (CAHMS)*

# INTRODUCTION

When I began researching for this book, my first fears were, how am I going to fill around 160 pages? My fears were unjustified; the problems were what to leave out and how to finish within the deadline for publication.

A number of decisions have had to be made, for instance whether to use the spelling Kyrton or Kirton – whichever I chose I knew it would be wrong in some people's eyes. Also when researching local businesses, sports clubs and societies, decisions had to be made on who to include and who not. I have tried to be fair but it is almost certain that someone or some group will have been missed who should have been included; if that is the case I can only apologise.

Throughout history Crediton has achieved importance and notoriety above and beyond that of a small market town. The town has been the seat of the Bishop of Devon and Cornwall, it has produced one of the most important missionary workers in the history of Europe, and it has been the seat of a soldier who was loved and respected at home and abroad (if not in Whitehall). The goods produced by the citizens of the town have historically been of a quality that has spread the name of Crediton far and wide. Today we have lost a little of our past status. We are no longer a market town, but we do still have industrial companies that are recognised around the world. One in five of our population may travel to Exeter to work each day, but there are still plenty who work and produce goods within the town, and there are also those who spread our name abroad through sporting achievements and through our societies and sports clubs.

## THE CREDITON AREA HISTORY AND MUSEUM SOCIETY

The Society was formed in 1984 by a group of enthusiastic local historians, their aim being to promote an interest in mainly local history and to provide Crediton with a museum. Since then it has put on a number of exhibitions covering subjects such as the Civil War, General Buller, a display of a replica of the Bayeaux Tapestry, and celebrating Queen Elizabeth II's golden jubilee with an exhibition about the 1950s. The Society also organises monthly meetings and occasional visits to local historical sites and buildings. Also, an archive of documents, maps and other artefacts is stored in rooms at Downes by kind permission of Mr Henry Parker.

*Spurway's Almshouses, Park Street, built out of monies bequeathed by Humphrey Spurway who died in 1555.*
(MRS W. DAVEY, PHOTO AUTHERS)

*'Rose Day' at Crediton, 1915.* (CAHMS, PHOTO BERRY)

# Chapter 1

# A Settlement by the Creedy

The first written reference to a settlement at or near where the town of Crediton now stands was in 739 when Aethelhard, King of Wessex, granted 'twenty hides of land in "Creedy"' to raise a monastery. However, it is reasonable to assume that there must have been a significant community here before that time. Indeed, Winfrith (later to become St Boniface) was said to be born here in or around the year 680. Also, the king was unlikely to have ordered a monastery to be raised on land unless there was an established settlement, and one that was capable of producing enough surplus food to support it. How long people had lived in the area prior to 739 is rather more difficult to establish. For many years it was thought that the Romans had advanced no further than Exeter, but in recent times there have been discoveries of Roman habitation as far west as Cornwall. Locally, sites have been discovered at Raddon and close to the Creedy between Crediton and Newton St Cyres. That said, neither of these locations are at Crediton.

It is, however, well established that the Saxons advanced into Devon in the seventh century, and the rich soil would have provided good natural pasture land in the marshy areas close to the River Creedy. It is quite possible that the original settlers came by sea

*Aerial photograph of the East Town, c.1930.* (PHOTO SIMMONS AEROFILMS)

rather than by land. The Exe would have been navigable by small boats above Exeter in those days, and the Creedy just possibly as far as Crediton. The first settlers would most probably have ventured upstream on foot. Indeed, it is said that the main reason why Leofric moved the Bishop's seat from Crediton to the walled city of Exeter in the eleventh century was fear of attack – by pirates. Also, the Saxons were said to favour river valleys rather than walled cities such as Exeter. Charles Luxton (former headmaster of Hayward's School) suggests that the original settlement would have been founded on slightly higher land away from the river to avoid any danger of flooding, which would place it somewhere near Tolleys and close to Lord's Meadow in the East Town of Crediton. He adds further weight to the argument for an earlier settlement, stating that a river crossing near to Creedy Bridge had been in existence 'since time immemorial'. This crossing may have been part of the main route to Cornwall since Roman times.

Luxton also points to the Saxon-type strip-field structure around the Lord's Meadow and Commonmarsh Lane area of the town. (An interesting aside to this is that these strip fields were often about 220 yards in length; a 'furrow long', hence a furlong.) Norden's 1598 map of Crediton gives clear evidence of such a field structure running down the hill from Commonmarsh Lane and from Old Tiverton Road down to Bramble Lane (now Exhibition Road). Most of the evidence for this has disappeared in recent years under housing and the industrial estate.

It is almost certain that early Crediton consisted only of the East Town. The valley running up to where the centre of the town now lies was probably almost impenetrable woodland in those early times with a small stream running down near to the settlement and on into the Creedy. This stream, later to become known as the Litterburn, ran through the valley and later the town until the nineteenth century, when it was filled in. Early maps of the town clearly show this stream and a lake in the centre of what is now Newcombes Meadow.

It is not known when the name Crediton was first used for the settlement here. The Creedy referred to in the document of 739 was almost certainly the name of a district or manor rather than the river. Prebendary J.F. Chanter, writing in 1922, suggested that the name has Celtic origins from the Celtic saint St Credan. If this is the case then it places the origins of the settlement in the sixth century at the latest, some 100 years before St Boniface. In the Domesday Book Crediton is called Critetona, but by 1200 the name Crediton seems to have been established. The name comes from the Saxon word 'tun' which means farm, thus Crediton; the farm by Creedy.

Crediton was clearly a well-recognised 'manor' by the time of the Domesday Book. Then the lord of the manor was the Bishop of Exeter, and he paid geld, or taxes, on 15 hides of land – land which was of sufficient quality for 185 ploughs to till. There was a mill, woodland five leagues in length and ½ a league in breadth (a league being about 1½ miles), 80 acres of meadow and 200 acres of pasture. He had some 400 serfs and villeins working this land, so if we add in wives, children and persons unable to work there must have been a relatively large population here in those times.

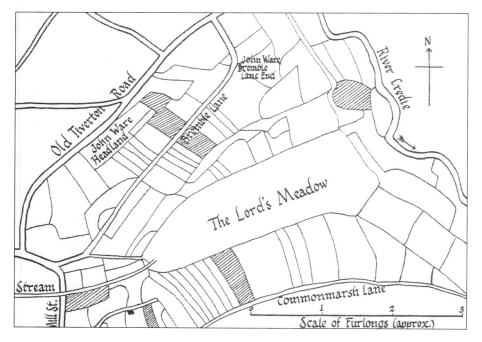

*Diagram of the East Town of Crediton as it was shown in Norden's Terrier of 1598. The strip fields along Commonmarsh Lane and Bramble Lane are clearly shown. The stream flowing into Lord's Meadow from the west is the Litterburn which was culverted in the nineteenth century. (CHARLES LUXTON)*

*View of the East Town taken from Downes Head before there were any buildings on Barnfield.*
*(CAHMS)*

*Crediton Girl Guides Guard of Honour awaiting the arrival of Princess Margaret for the unveiling of the*
*St Boniface statue in 1960.  (PHOTO AUTHERS)*

It is not certain when the town began to expand up the valley to the west, but it is possible to conclude that the five-league narrow strip of woodland mentioned in Domesday could well be that valley. The earliest reference we have to the West Town is in 1242, when Bishop Brewer of Exeter speaks of 'our new borough of Crediton'. Around this time King Henry III granted a weekly market and a three-day fair at 'St Laurence tide'. St Lawrence Chapel was certainly in existence by that date, as also was the nearby leper colony and burial-ground of St Lawrence Green.

So why did Crediton, rather than any of the other settlements in the area, grow from a small community into a prosperous market town? This is an impossible question to answer with certainty, but we do know that the land was and still is particularly fertile. Also, being the site of an established river crossing, which may or may not have been on the main route into Cornwall, would have been a contributory factor. However, almost certainly the main reason was that Crediton had the advantage of an established monastic community which later, as we will see, developed into the cathedral seat of Devon and Cornwall, and later still a collegiate church. Such an establishment would have required a relatively large population to support it. This already established population would have, during the early-medieval period, further grown and prospered as the market town for agriculture and the wool industry in central Devon.

*The Crediton Seal. Unfortunately, it has not been possible to trace the significance of the date 1469. (CREDITON TOWN COUNCIL)*

# Chapter 2

# St Boniface: The Greatest Englishman

*The Blue Plaque in Tolleys marking the probable birthplace of St Boniface.*

The seventh century was a violent age and, spending his early years in a disputed land, the young Winfrith is likely to have witnessed much bloodshed and violence. According to his biographer, Willibald, he came from a landed and possibly even a noble family, and his early religious inspiration may well have come from the visiting monks and preachers who would have stayed with the family. He was said to be his father's favourite son and he intended him for a secular life, but the young Winfrith was determined to follow a religious path, some say from as early as four or five years of age. He was possibly as young as ten when he walked to the Benedictine Abbey at Exeter to study under Abbot Wolfhard, but he did not remain there long. When he reached manhood he found the teaching at Exeter inadequate and moved on to the Abbey of Nursling (between Winchester and Southampton) to further his religious education.

V irtually every schoolchild in Crediton will have been taught about St Boniface, but you will not need to venture far from the town within the UK to find that the saint of which Crediton is justly proud is virtually unheard of. Yet if you travel to mainland Europe his fame is widespread, especially in Holland where he was martyred, and Germany where he is a patron saint of the country. Boniface is also the patron saint of brewers, tailors and file-cutters.

There is no direct evidence that St Boniface was born in Crediton. Indeed the earliest written record comes from Bishop Grandisson of Exeter in the fourteenth century, some 600 years after Boniface's martyrdom. However, as we will see, the town's claim to its most famous son is well founded. It is widely accepted that Winfrith (or Wynfrith or Winfrid) was born in the year 680, although a few scholars place his birth as much as ten years before that. The name Winfrith comes from the Saxon language and means joy (Wyn) and peace (Frith). It is known that the area in which he was born was on the frontier between the Saxon and British kingdoms.

*The statue of St Boniface in Newcombes Meadow.*
*(CAHMS)*

He prospered at Nursling and was ordained a priest at the age of 30. His reputation within the Church in England grew and a good career was forecast for him. However, Winfrith felt that his calling was for missionary work, and in 716 he was sent to Frisia in Holland. Christianity had already reached that area and so he expected it to be a fruitful place to spread the word. However, political disturbances and other problems caused him to return to England. His first missionary expedition, therefore, resulted in failure.

Winfrith was not deterred. He was offered the position of abbot at Nursling on the death of his tutor Winbert, but refused the promotion as he wished to return to missionary work. He made his first visit to Rome in 718, where Pope Gregory II authorised him to preach the Gospel to the heathens in Germany 'to the right of the Rhine'. He found the Church flourishing in southern parts of Germany, especially Bavaria, but the north of the country, although having previously been converted to Christianity, had reverted to pagan practices. He met with some success and in 722 the Pope asked him to return to Rome to report on his progress. Gregory was impressed and consecrated him a regional bishop, giving him the name Boniface; Boniface being the Latin translation of Winfrith.

On his return he found that the Germans had drifted back into paganism. In order to provide an example of the weakness of the pagan Gods in the face of the Christian God, Boniface felled the sacred oak of Thor at Geismar and had a chapel built out of its timbers. Tradition has it that the locals were so astonished that Thor had not sent a thunderbolt to strike him down many were converted to Christianity on the spot.

In 732 he was made an archbishop by Pope Gregory III, with instructions to appoint bishops as he thought necessary. For the next 20 years of his life he based himself at Fulda, but spent the majority of his time in missionary work. He did, however, spend time at the Fulda monastery training the monks, and in prayer and meditation. However, he did have one outstanding omission to rectify; his first failed mission to convert the Frisians. In 754 he resigned the archbishopric and commenced a missionary tour of that region. By this time he was at least 74 years of age, so this undertaking must have been hard for him. At Dokkum, on the River Borne, heathens fell upon him and his companions in the night and slaughtered some 52 persons. Boniface, it is said, held the Bible above his head to protect himself. (Some scholars claim that he was holding the Gospels.) His body was eventually taken to his monastery in Fulda where he was buried.

Boniface never returned to the place of his birth after leaving it at such an early age, and as far as we know never again met his parents – this would not have been too unusual for someone choosing a monastic life. Some 150 of his letters survive; much of this correspondence was with popes, kings and princes, and he was not afraid to criticise anyone, no matter how important, if he felt they were straying from the ways of Christianity. Some letters also survive that were written shortly after his death which praise his work; in particular one from the then Archbishop of Canterbury, Cuthbert. Unfortunately none of them refer to his birth at Crediton.

Why then can Crediton make a strong claim to be his birthplace? If we refer back to the previous chapter dealing with the origins of the town there is evidence of a substantial settlement in the area by the time Winfrith was born. We also know he was born of 'well-to-do parents' who lived in such a settlement and, as far as we know, other than Exeter, there was nowhere else of that size in the area at that time. Also, it cannot be mere coincidence that a monastery was founded at Crediton in 739 at the height of his missionary work in Germany, and a substantial religious community existed for the whole of the intervening period, until Grandisson's claim some 600 years later. As Charles Luxton states in his pamphlet written in 1955:

> *... it is hardly conceivable that the birth-place of such a man as St. Boniface, so famous during his lifetime and so glorious in his martyrdom, would ever have been lost sight of in his native town.*

So, whilst there is no written evidence to confirm the fact, neither is there any surviving documentation from that era to disprove it. The evidence may be circumstantial, but to quote Luxton again, 'It is precisely the way in which tradition accords so closely with the known facts of the case that makes it of rather more than purely local interest.'

## St Boniface and the Christmas Tree

According to tradition, when Boniface chopped down the pagan oak at Geismar a tiny tree was growing in its roots. It was a small evergreen fir and from that time it became a symbol of Christ among the German peoples. Over time the tradition spread around the world and eventually became a symbol of Christmas.

## St Boniface Celebrations

There are no records of anniversary celebrations prior to the nineteenth century, but since then significant dates have been remembered. In 1954 the 1200th anniversary of his martyrdom was marked with church services and a walk over the believed route he took between Crediton and Exeter when he went to the monastery as a very young man. These celebrations were attended by Dr Fisher, the Archbishop of Canterbury. In 1980 the 1300th anniversary of his birth was marked by a visit from HRH Princess Alexandra. In June 2004 further celebrations were held in Crediton and across Europe to mark the 1250th anniversary of his martyrdom. Also, on and around his saint's day, 11 June, Crediton receives a significant number of visitors from both Dokkum and Fulda.

In 1960 the late Princess Margaret visited the town to unveil the statue which stands in Newcombes Meadow. There was an unfortunate incident when the drape that covered the statue failed to fall away when the Princess pulled the cord, and despite the efforts of several people it would not budge. Eventually, two local Scouts came to the rescue and the drape was hauled off the statue in a rather unceremonious manner. The story behind this occurrence is that the drape had become torn a few days before the event and had to be hurriedly repaired. In the early hours of the day of the unveiling, workmen arrived to enclose the statue in the drape and to take down the scaffolding. Unfortunately they could not remember how to properly tie the 'slip knot' that would allow the drape to fall freely, the result being that when the Princess pulled the cord nothing happened. An addition to this story is that when, many years later, some Crediton people had to go to London to meet the Princess, she is reported to have remarked that she remembered Crediton as 'the place the drape would not fall down.'

Although Boniface may not be widely remembered in the country of his birth, his contribution to the spread of Christianity is widely acknowledged on the Continental mainland, so much so that there is talk of him being made the patron saint of the EU.

Left to right: *Les Matanle, Ron Avery, the Bishop of Exeter, Wilfred Westall (Bishop of Crediton), and Revd Anthony Bray accompanying the late Princess Margaret into Crediton Parish Church, 1960. (CAHMS)*

*Crowds awaiting the arrival of Princess Margaret, 1960.* (PHOTO AUTHERS)

# Chapter 3

# The Church of the Holy Cross
## and the Mother of Him Who Hung Thereon

*'When Kirton was a cathedral town, Exeter was but a fuzzy down'*

This little rhyme, or variations on it, has been handed down through generations of Kirtonians. However, it is not strictly correct. Yes, Crediton was considered of sufficient importance in the tenth century, by the Church at least, to be granted the Diocese of Devon; but to class Exeter as a 'fuzzy down' at that time was a bit of an exaggeration, as it was an established city surrounded by walls built by the Romans and recently restored by Alfred the Great. In some ways this adds to the importance of Crediton, for it was chosen above its well-established near neighbour.

Since the very earliest of times Crediton has been a religious community, for the young Winfrith had been raised in an environment where monks and preachers were regular visitors. Also, in 739, the King of Wessex thought the settlement of sufficient importance to pay for the establishment of a monastery.

In 909 Plegmund, the Archbishop of Canterbury, decided to reorganise the Diocese of Wessex which was administered from Winchester, by splitting it into smaller units. Crediton was awarded the Diocese of Devon. Whether this was because of the surviving reputation of St Boniface, or the importance of the monastery, or the size of the settlement, is unclear. The first bishop to be consecrated was Eadwulf, and in all there were ten Bishops at Crediton over a period of 141 years. Around 1040 a further reorganisation took place and Crediton also became the seat of the Bishop of Cornwall. In 1050 the last bishop, Leofric, transferred the see to Exeter where it has remained ever since.

The eleventh century was a violent time, and Wessex was still disputed land. However, the greatest risk at that time was from Danish pirates who rowed up the Exe and then continued on foot up the Creedy to raid the town; further evidence of the wealth and importance of Crediton in those times. Leofric saw the walled city of Exeter as a much safer and more easily defended place. The loss of cathedral status must have been a bitter blow to Crediton.

Who can say what the size and importance of our town would have been if the bishop's seat had remained here.

**BISHOPS OF CREDITON**

| | |
|---|---|
| *Eadwulf* | *909–34* |
| *Æthelgar* | *934–53* |
| *Æfweald I* | *953–72* |
| *Sideman* | *973–77* |
| *Ælfric* | *977–85* |
| *Æfweald II* | *985–88* |
| *Æfweald III* | *988–1008* |
| *Eadnoth* | *1008–27* |
| *Leofing or Lyfing\** | *1027–46* |
| *Leofric\** | *1046–50* |

*\* Also Bishop of Cornwall*
(SOURCE: POWICKE AND FRYDE, 1961)

The cathedral was dedicated to St Gregory, but no remains of it have ever been found. There have been archaeological excavations but to no avail, because the building was almost certainly constructed of wood. It is thought to have been situated a little behind and to the east of the present church building, probably near the house called 'The Palace'.

Few records remain of the church at Crediton for the 200 years following Leofric's removal to Exeter, but it must have remained active as in 1253 there is a reference to a College of Canons, which seems to have been well established. This college consisted of 18 canons, 12 of whom were prebends (a prebend is land attached to a church from which a priest obtains his living). These 12 prebends were Woolsgrove, Poole, Henstill, Stawford, Aller, Rudge, Woodland, Kerswell, Priestcombe, Cross, West Sandford and Creedy. (The name Creedy does not refer to the river, but to land probably in the Upton Hellions area.) Some of these names survive to this day in the parishes of Crediton and Sandford. The Prebend of

*Work in progress on the archaeological dig in 1991 in an area which is now the church car park. The dig failed to find the site of the Saxon cathedral, but revealed many interesting items, including the foundations of cottages demolished in the nineteenth century.*
(CREDITON COUNTRY COURIER)

Poole was the 'town' prebend and consisted of land near the church, part of which was almost certainly Newcombes Meadow. The Poole prebend also possessed a large house which stood just to the north or north-west of the church. The prebendary canons survived until the Reformation.

During the thirteenth and fourteenth centuries the college seems to have been either unable or unwilling to maintain the church buildings in a state of decent repair, for Bishop Grandisson of Exeter reported in 1334 that the building had 'become ruinous'. Nothing was done for almost a century until in 1413 William Langton left a sum of money to rebuild the church which, in his words, had become 'nearly levelled to the ground'. There are similar reports in 1511 and in 1523 when Bishop Veysey described the church as 'advancing towards desolation'.

*The Chapter House, one of the few parts of the church fabric to survive the neglect of the fourteenth and fifteenth centuries. (CAHMS, BARNES SERIES)*

Some 20 years later, however, a great deal of restoration work seems to have been completed, for John Leland, on visiting Crediton in 1545, reported that 'the Church hath no manner or token of antiquity', in other words it looked almost new. Indeed the building that Leland saw probably looked quite similar to that which stands in 2004. Parts of the present building date back to the twelfth century, and the Lady Chapel and Chapter House are thirteenth-century in origin, but there is little else that has survived those 200 years of neglect.

There was one notable event during this period when the 'Miracle of Crediton' occurred. On 1 August 1315 it was reported that Thomas Orey recovered his sight before the altar of St Nicholas.

The collegiate church survived until 1547 when it was dissolved by decree of Edward VI. It was originally scheduled for demolition by order of his father Henry VIII, but the buildings were saved from that fate by the zeal of the local townspeople who raised the sum of £200 (estimated to be £50,000 of today's money).

*A photograph showing the north side of the Collegiate Church of the Holy Cross and the Mother of Him Who Hung Thereon. Most images of the Parish Church are taken from the south side.*
(CAHMS, PHOTO AUTHERS)

Edward VI's charter, dated 2 April 1547, vests authority over the hereditaments and goods of the church in the hands of 12 governors in perpetuity. This authority extends to the parish of Sandford, and for some unexplained reason also to Exminster. The governors were all to be inhabitants of the parish, nine of Crediton and three of Sandford. These governors were responsible for the church buildings, the graveyard, the vicar's house and the school-house. The governors also had in their power the appointment of the vicar (now rector) of Crediton and his or her assistants. This authority was confirmed in a further charter of 5 July 1559 during the reign of Elizabeth I. The Queen further decreed that the salary of the vicar should be £30 per annum, the chaplain £10, and the master of the Grammar School £13.6s.8d. (£13.33), with houses to be provided for them. James I doubled the vicar's salary in 1625. However, in 1808 the then vicar John Rudall, along with the vicar of Exminster, filed a case in the Court of Chancery against the governors, and after lengthy litigation his stipend was increased to £400.

The 12 governors are a self-perpetuating body, and when one dies or leaves the parish, the remaining 11 elect a successor. These charters have never been repealed and to this day the Church of England in Crediton and Sandford is run by 12 governors.

Over the centuries many of the governors have been local landowners. Indeed, William Pope, writing in 1927, suggested that being a landowner, and thus liable to pay tithes, would make a person more likely 'to be careful in the management of parochial affairs.' The first governors included John Bodleigh, Robert Trobridge, Robert Davey and Robert Holcombe. In 1624, in addition to the surnames listed above, the names of Sir William Killigrew, Emanuel Davie and John Tuckfield were amongst the 12. In 1852 the governors were: Sir Humphrey Ferguson Davie Bart, James Wentworth Buller, J.H. Hippisley, P. Francis, D. Tremlett, E.T. Ward, J. Yarde, B. Cleave, B.W. Cleave, William Pope, E. Norris and Edwin Empson. Many of these names are still recognisable in the town at the time of writing. In 1996 Mrs Helen Lawes was appointed as a governor, breaking a tradition of some 450 years in which only men were elected to the office.

Few towns the size of Crediton can boast such an impressive church building. It dominates the East Town, which, given its history it surely should. It is built of local stone taken from now-disused quarries at Posbury and Knowle. It is cruciform in shape, with a massive central tower which rises to almost 100 feet (30 metres). The tower contains a peal of eight bells, seven of which were cast in 1774. The tenor bell is dated 1814. At the time of writing these bells are in a poor state of repair. In December 2002 the clapper of the tenor bell, which weighs 28 cwt, broke away from its housing. In 2004 an appeal is under way for the repair and restoration of the bells, and although at the time of writing the full amount required has not yet been achieved, sufficient monies have been donated for work to start.

The north chancel contains a magnificent, recently restored, organ which was originally installed in 1921.

It is a memorial to a former organist, who was appropriately named Harold Charles Organ, and who was killed in the First World War. To the east end there is a Lady Chapel, which once served as the Grammar School and is possibly built over part of the original cathedral building. The Chapter House on the south side of the building, which now houses the vestry and above it the Governors' Room, is probably the oldest part of the building, being one of the few areas to have largely survived the neglect of the thirteenth and fourteenth centuries.

## VICARS OF CREDITON SINCE THE REFORMATION

| | |
|---|---|
| Peter Duncan | 1583–95 |
| William Cooke | 1595–1616 |
| Richard Coles | 1616–50 |
| John Dicker | 1650–89 |
| Thomas Ley | 1689–1721 |
| Robert Ham | 1721–31 |
| John Carwithen | 1731–42 |
| John Stacy | 1742–59 |
| Samuel Hart | 1759–93 |
| John Rudall | 1793–1835 |
| Samuel Rowe | 1835–54 |
| Charles Felton Smith | 1854–1901 |
| Walter Smith-Dorien | 1901–25 |
| Humphrey Onslow | 1925–29 |
| John Durling | 1929–40 |
| Francis Richards | 1940–53 |
| Anthony Bray | 1953–75 |
| Bruce Duncan | 1975–86 |
| Anthony Geering | 1986–2002 |
| Nigel Guthrie | 2002– |

The church contains a number of monuments, the most impressive of which is that to General Sir Redvers Buller. Other notable monuments are to John Tuckfield of Tedburn and Fulford, Sir William Perriam, and Sir John Sully.

Extensive work was undertaken on the interior of the building in the years immediately following 1887 to commemorate Queen Victoria's golden jubilee. According to Revd Smith-Dorien:

*... the whole of the hideous box pews, which had been erected of every possible size, and facing in every direction, were swept away, and replaced by oak seats with carved ends, whilst the old flooring was entirely removed, and replaced by Italian mosaic work in the chancel and tile or wood paving elsewhere.*

*The disfiguring galleries were removed, and the beauty of the interior, long hidden by excrescences in worst of taste, was once more disclosed.*

The richly carved chancel stalls were supplied by Mr William Dart, and the lectern was presented by Mr John Mortimer, a church governor. The font is considered to be Norman, but the elaborate oak cover, designed by M.D. Caroe, was presented in 1908 in memory of William Dart, by his family. By this time the interior of the church must have looked very much like it does in 2004, the only notable change since then being the addition of an altar between the choir and the nave.

During the Second World War some damage was caused to the north side of the building and the clock face by a stray German bomb which fell in a nearby field.

*Revd Felton Smith (centre) with Verger Bill Wollacott. The man on the right is unknown. The Wollacott family were sextons and gravediggers for generations. The wife of Bill's father (also called Bill) was the church cleaner and before the wooden floor was installed she would have had to scrub the whole stone floor of the church every week.* (Margaret Wollacott)

## St Lawrence Chapel

The first mention of St Lawrence Chapel was in 1242. It was almost certainly constructed to serve a nearby leper hospital. If, indeed, this was the reason for the building of the chapel, we can conclude that the West Town of Crediton was not developed by this time, as a leper colony would almost certainly have been built away from places of habitation.

The site was probably chosen for its proximity to the Litterburn which flowed through the town, and possibly alongside an ancient road leading up the valley and on to the west.

St Lawrence was a very early Christian martyr. He was a deacon of the Roman Church and in 258, and following an edict by the Emperor Sixtus which commanded that all officers of the Church should be put to death, he was burned on a grid iron. He was chosen as the patron saint of this and several other leper hospitals.

Brother Nicholas, a Trinitarian monk and hermit, was the first to live in a hermitage along-side the chapel, and would almost certainly have looked after the hospital and its inmates. This situation continued under several generations of monks until the sixteenth century when the chapel came under the authority of the church governors when they were established in 1547. Some time after this the roof of the chapel was stripped of its lead, and the shell of the building was left in ruins for centuries.

At some stage it was converted into a cottage, but in 1920/21 it was restored to a chapel by the architect Sir Charles Nicholson. The building had been purchased by Mrs Drake of Winswood with a view to restoring it as a memorial to her husband Henry Drake.

## Millenary Celebrations, 1909

A great celebration was held in 1909 to mark 1,000 years since the first Bishop of Crediton. The Archbishop of Canterbury attended and a throne was specially constructed for him by the craftsmen of Dart & Francis.

Admission to the event was by invitation or ticket only and this proved to be a wise precaution, as with the church full there was a large gathering at every gate to the churchyard at least half an hour before the service was due to start. The service was followed by tea on the vicarage lawn.

The programme for the event included the following paragraph, praising the glorious history of the town:

*One thousand years ago – centuries before the history of the United States and Australia commenced, and when towns like Birmingham and Barrow-in-Furness were non-existent – Crediton was a place of note, and had been for more than 200 years.*

Left: *Churchwarden Alison Hulland presents a painting by James Charlwood of Crediton Parish Church to Revd Anthony Gearing upon his retirement in 2002. The photo was taken after his final service at Holy Trinity Church, Yeoford.* (CREDITON COUNTRY COURIER)

Right: *Clergy and choir in 1906.* (CREDITON CHURCH GOVERNORS)

*Internal view of St Lawrence Chapel shortly after renovations were completed in the early years of the twentieth century.* (CAHMS)

*Clergy gathering for the 1909 millenary celebrations and awaiting the arrival of the Archbishop of Canterbury.  Note the false frontage on part of the church.  (CAHMS, PHOTO BERRY).*

## The Governor's Helmet

### By Robin Langhorne

The Italianate helmet, kept in the Governors' Room in the Church of the Holy Cross in Crediton is a fake. A fake is much more interesting than a copy since there is almost always a story of human wrongdoing in the former, and thus it proves to be in this instance.

In 1910, the governors sent the original helmet away to be refurbished by Mr A.L. Radford of Beer. This gentleman took it to a meeting of the Armourers in London and lent it to one Samuel Whawell, an amateur collector and craftsman in metal.  It was apparently returned to Mr Radford and ultimately to Crediton Church, where it once more hung in the Governors' Room.  In 1940, an article which appeared in the local press casting doubt on the authenticity of the helmet was refuted by the governors and its untroubled provenance continued until 1957 when an apparently identical helmet was bequeathed to the Philadelphia Museum of Art.

Much detective work was done, particularly by Claude Blair.  In 1927, after the death of Samuel Whawell, his effects, including one of the helmets, were put on sale.  The latter was purchased by the agent of William Randolph Hearst, who sold it in 1941 to Otto von Kiebusch, and it was he who bequeathed the helmet to the Philadelphia Museum in 1957. Expert armourers now knew of the existence of two helmets, identical even to the rust holes.  An assay of the metal was carried out and the Crediton version was found to be a fake.  Plainly, Samuel

Whawell was the culprit and his acquisitive nature has left us with an object of only limited value but a very good story.

Attempts were made to recover the original, but since it had been sold twice in good faith and bequeathed once, neither English nor American law had the power to restore it to its one-time owners.

*The fake Italianate helmet.
(CREDITON CHURCH GOVERNORS)*

## A Find of Coins

In 1896 the first-floor room of the Chapter House was converted into a robing room for the church choir. This room is immediately below the one where the governors meet.  As part of the renovation a plaster ceiling which had been fixed many years before was removed.  This revealed a rough set of pigeon-holes at one end of the room where a workman discovered an embroidered leather bag.  This bag contained a number of silver coins (it was said a total of 1884) dating from the reign of Henry VII through to James II.

According to Lt Col Montague, writing in the early part of the twentieth century, the bag with its contents weighed almost 20 pounds. The dates of these coins cover the Reformation period, up to a time just prior to the enthronement of William III and Mary II as monarchs, and the settlement of the Church of England as the established church.

We cannot know for sure what happened or why these coins were hidden, but it is quite possible that either the treasurer or clerk of the governors hid them to avoid them falling into the wrong hands. For whatever reason, the person who left them there never returned, and they remained hidden for over 200 years.

The lord of the manor of Crediton, Sir Redvers Buller, claimed the find on behalf of the town, as did the church governors, but a coroner's inquest pronounced the find to be 'treasure trove' and therefore the property of the Crown. Lt Col Montague informed us that the British Museum kept 13 coins for the 'national collection' and General Buller kept sufficient to cover a silver cigar box. 'The remainder were returned to the church governors who sold them by auction, rewarding the finder out of the proceeds.' The auction, held at the Town Hall in May 1897, raised a sum of around £100.

## The Prayer Book Rebellion, 1549

The rebellion occurred in the early years of the Church of England, at a time when many people, especially in the West Country, still preferred the Roman Catholic ritual. However, the 1549 Act of Unification made it illegal, from Whit Sunday, to conduct Mass in Latin.

The rebellion started in the village of Sampford Courtenay, but one of the most significant encounters of the whole uprising was 'The Affair of the Crediton Barns.' It seems that the new service had been read on Whit Sunday at Sampford Courtenay, as it was in every other parish, with very little trouble. However, on the following day the people of that village forced the local priest to don 'his old popish attire' and conduct the service in Latin. News of this disturbance soon spread, and it seems people joined in from many nearby villages and marched towards Crediton. The town seems to have been the rallying point for the rebels, for they were soon to be joined by groups from Cornwall.

News of the uprising reached King Edward VI and he sent two Devon men, Sir Peter and Sir Gawen Carew, to deal with the rebels. The two knights rode to Crediton to reason with them, but on reaching the town found the roads blocked by trenches and fortified ramparts. They found it impossible to proceed or to negotiate with the rebels.

The rebels had armed men hidden in nearby barns, but in the face of musket fire the King's men set fire to the barns and the rebels retreated into the town. The Carews thought this was the end of the rebellion and withdrew back to Exeter. However, more reinforcements soon arrived in Crediton from Cornwall, where support for the old style of service was widespread. The strengthened rebel band marched on Exeter and laid siege to the West Gate of the city for five weeks.

Eventually the King raised an army under the command of Lord John Russell, which marched on Exeter fighting heavy battles at Feniton and Bishop's Clyst. Once Russell's army reached Exeter the revolt was effectively over and the rebels were driven back past the burnt barns at Crediton where many were either taken prisoner or killed. Over 4,000 lives were lost in the rebellion.

## Crediton During the Civil War

Crediton saw a good deal of action during the Civil War with both sides holding the town at differing periods. However, the town did avoid being the scene of a battle. It supported the King for much of the war, being secure for Charles until late in 1645.

Prince Maurice's army was quartered here during a significant part of 1644, but the Cavalier diarist Richard Symonds did not think much of Crediton, describing it as 'a big lousy town'. Maurice was forced to retreat for a short while but soon returned to have his troops reviewed by King Charles on 27 July at Lord's Meadow.

In October 1645 Sir Robert Fairfax took possession of the town on behalf of the Parliamentarian cause, and remained here for three months. The town then became the Parliamentarians' headquarters and Cromwell reviewed his troops at the same site where the King had performed a similar activity just over 12 months earlier.

All the soldiers, but particularly the Royalists, were hated in the town because they demanded board and lodgings but did not feel a need to pay.

*A saddle left behind by a soldier (probably an officer) during the Civil War. The saddle is kept in the Governors' Room.*
*(CREDITON CHURCH GOVERNORS)*

*The Archbishop of Canterbury at the millenary celebrations of 1909.*
*(CAHMS, PHOTO BERRY)*

*The Archbishop of Canterbury's procession at the celebrations held to mark the 1,000th anniversary of the installation of the first Bishop of Crediton in 909. (CAHMS, PHOTO BERRY)*

*An etching showing the Sexton's House, c.1820. This house was the end one of a range of four which were demolished later in the nineteenth century, along with a similar range to the east, to provide additional burial room at the rear of the churchyard. The houses stood parallel to Church Street and would have stood across the cobbled path which now runs from Church Street to Church Lane at the rear of the churchyard and encroached on the area that is now the car park for the Boniface Centre. The other houses in the west range were the clink and an infants' school. The east range was mainly used as a Sunday school. The grave surrounded by iron railings still stands in the churchyard, but the railings have been removed. In those days the verger was William Wollacott and when the houses were demolished he was rehoused at No. 13 Church Street. (MARGARET WOLLACOTT)*

*The clergy and choir in 1969:* Left to right, back row: *George Sheppard, Francis Bray, Jo Ward, Derek Hubbard, Phil Trenaman, Ray Foden, Jim Ward, Roy Steadman, Walter Hosegood;* fourth row: *Gillian Foden, Kath Symonds, Dorothy Sheppard, Charlotte Daniel, Gillian Bashford, Muriel Foden, Marjorie Padwick, Janet Sheppard, Ruth Saunders, Kitty Ward;* third row: *E. Rich, A. Wingrave-Paine, Jenny Wilson, Cathy Padwick, Jane Trenaman, Liz Sheppard, Janet Minter, P. Young, Alison Foden, Marjorie Brown;* second row: *Jean Foden, David Parr, Richard Cope, David Way, Chris Samuel, Pete Langhorne, Geoff Selwood, S. Burridge;* front row: *Revd Vic House, Revd Ted Littlejohn, Revd Anthony Bray, Rt Revd Wilfred Westall (Bishop of Crediton), Dr John Powell, Revd Robin Turner, Henry Brinkworth.*

(CREDITON CHURCH GOVERNORS, PHOTO HIGH STREET STUDIOS)

*East Street looking towards the town. The sign on the wall in the background reads 'Crediton Steam Laundry'. The building was originally Elston's Boot Factory, and since then it has been a garage and a plant-hire company.*
*(CAHMS)*

*St Lawrence Green. (CAHMS)*

*A funeral courtége arrives at the Parish Church. We don't know who's funeral it was, but, judging by the crowd, the deceased must have been fairly important. (CAHMS)*

*Crediton Parish Church. (CAHMS, PHOTO BERRY)*

# Chapter 4

# Catholics and Dissenters in Crediton

## Catholicism Since the Reformation

For hundreds of years following the Reformation, Roman Catholics in Crediton, as in most other towns, met in secret in private houses. It was not until the First World War that they became more open and organised in their worship. In 1914 Canon Shepherd, a parish priest from Exeter, came to the town by train each Sunday to say Mass at the Town Hall and to attend to the needs of Catholic soldiers in the two military hospitals in the town. At that time there were only about 14 Crediton residents who were Catholics.

After the war the former Methodist Chapel on Bowden Hill was rented and regular services were held there. In 1928 the Church bought the building and refurbished it. Since then there has been a regular place of worship for Catholics in Crediton.

The opportunity of regular worship on a permanent site meant that the congregation continued to grow in strength until, on 3 October 1969, a new church, in Park Street, was opened and blessed by the Bishop of Plymouth, Cyril Restieaux. This new church was founded largely due to the efforts of Dom John Stephan, a Benedictine Monk from Buckfast Abbey. Father Stephan had devoted much of his life's work to St Boniface (who was also a Benedictine) and was instrumental in raising money towards the building of the church in the birthplace of the saint. He used the Fulda connection to obtain donations from bishops in Germany.

Father George Hay was appointed chaplain to the University of Exeter in 1966, and also priest-in-charge at Crediton. He was to become heavily involved with the building of the new church. The contract was awarded to local builders Berry & Vincent and work started in October 1968. The foundation-stone was donated by the Bishop of Fulda.

The church building is divided into three interconnected sections – an area for worship; the shrine of St Boniface and the Meeting Room. The St Boniface shrine, a national shrine, was designed by Kenneth Carter, and depicts the felling of the oak tree at Geismar.

When the church was consecrated on 3 October 1980 the revival of Catholicism in the town of Crediton could be said to have been nearly completed. The congregation had grown from just 14 to almost 250. In 2004 there is one further step to be achieved, and that is for Crediton to no longer be part of the parish of Exeter, but to be recognised as a parish in its own right.

## The Bowden Hill Meeting-House
*By Mary Blamey*

Until the mid-1960s Crediton contained what was believed to be the largest single-span cob building in the country. This was the Unitarian Church, which displayed the date 1729 on its vestry ceiling and was built on the hill dividing the East and West Towns.

Previous to this the Presbyterians of Kirton (as they were then known) had worshipped in a small cob building (previously a barn) approached by a passage between Nos. 107 and 108 High Street. But during the ministry of Josiah Eveleigh the new building was erected mostly at the expense of the Davie family, who also supplied the two fine oak pillars that supported the interior roof. It was a typical simple Dissenting meeting-house, being wider than it was long with a pulpit (with a sounding-board above) facing the entrance and two galleries. On the rear wall near the pulpit was a parliament clock and an organ was housed in one of the galleries. However, the Davie family ceased their support on the succession of the 5th baronet in 1728 and began their affinity with Sandford Parish Church. At the time of its greatest prosperity in 1715 the chapel was estimated to have 600 hearers.

A doctrinal split at Bowden Hill came about in the time of Revd Miciah Towgood. He was at Crediton some years before espousing Presbyterian Unitarianism as against Presbyterian Trinitarianism, in which he carried the greater part of the congregation, and as the property was attached in no recorded tenets the majority party remained in possession. The lease of the old chapel in the High Street had passed to John Welsford and Samuel Hooker, both prominent Dissenters, and it may be that the Trinitarians, apprehensive as to where their leaders were leading them, decided not to go with the majority to the 'New Meeting-House' but to remain in the old quarters and later become the Congregational Church.

The site chosen for this interesting building was, however, to prove its downfall. A row of cottages below the church had to be demolished and nothing was done to replace the support they had been giving to the hill. As a result the side of the hill began to move, taking the church with it and causing its walls to crack, with fatal results. There was time before the demise of the building for the members to disperse some of the internal fittings. The clock is at Moretonhampstead Unitarian Church, the organ in the Manse at Dundee, and the pulpit was reconstructed for use at Horsham Unitarian Church in Essex, who also accepted the font, but the oak panelling was used to enclose the Lady Chapel in Crediton Parish Church. The Eveleigh Flats stand on this site in 2004.

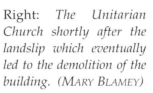

Left: *The interior of the Unitarian Church.*

Right: *The Unitarian Church shortly after the landslip which eventually led to the demolition of the building. (*MARY BLAMEY*)*

*The Unitarian Church, c.1900. (*MARY BLAMEY, PHOTO BERRY*)*

*Early photograph of the Congregational Church and Manse. (CAHMS, KNIGHT COLLECTION)*

*The Congregational Church decorated for Harvest Festival. (MARGARET WOLLACOTT)*

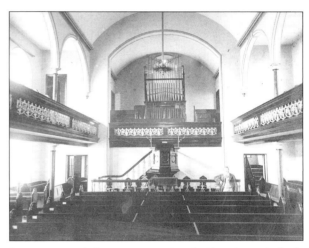

*The interior of the Congregational Church as it looked prior to the alterations of 1998. (MARGARET WOLLACOTT)*

## Crediton Congregational Church

The founders of the Congregational Church seceded from the Unitarians, who worshipped at the Bowden Hill Chapel, in 1756. For the first year of their separate existence they met in private houses, but by the following year they had established a meeting-house in Broad Street, behind what is now Nos. 107 and 108 High Street. The building has long gone, but evidence of the burial-ground remains in the garden behind this property with gravestones lining the walls and at the back, steps which once led up to a very small chapel building. The first minister was Samuel Buncombe.

Exactly a century later, in 1856, this building had become too small to hold a growing congregation. Therefore, under the then minister, William Snell, a larger site was purchased some 100 yards further up the High Street. Money had to be raised for the building and it was not until March 1863 that the foundation-stone was laid. Francis Channon, a local builder, was chosen to do the main construction work. In fact local craftsmen were used to undertake all of the work. The new chapel was completed the following year but the old one remained as a Sunday school until at least 1878, and quite possibly later. In 1890 a new Manse and Sunday school were built alongside the chapel.

For many years the Congregational Church fête was a major social event in the town. In the early-twentieth century it was held at Belle Meadow, but later moved to Fordton House, home of photographer Mr Authers. In 1964 the last fête was held at Fordton; Mr Authers died the following year, ending a long association with the church.

Nationally, the Congregational churches underwent reform in the late 1960s, and there was lengthy debate as to whether Crediton would join the new United Reform Church. In 1971 the members voted against union.

On 16 April 1977, Sir Cliff Richard sang at the church. It was reported that his visit was 'appreciated by people of all ages' and the event raised a considerable sum for local charities.

Throughout most of the twentieth century membership remained around the 100 mark, but by the 1980s this number had begun to fall and the church was beginning to struggle financially. Indeed, the Revd Goldie left in 1987, convinced that the Congregational Church had no future in Crediton.

In 1998 there was further controversy, over changes to the inside of the building. The debate was whether or not to remove the fixed pews in the downstairs area in order that it may be used for purposes other than religious services. The reason behind this was partly financial as membership, and therefore income, was still falling. This proposal caused a great deal of controversy. Those in favour of change won the day, but at a cost, as some members left the church.

## Wesleyan Methodism

The first followers of John Wesley worshipped in a room on the ground floor of a house in Dean Street owned by Mr Samuel Laimbeer. The room was first licensed in 1808 and a local preacher, Mr Ryan, conducted those early meetings. At that time Crediton was part of the Exeter circuit.

The congregation quickly grew in strength and in 1815 work started on the chapel at the top of Bowden Hill. This is the same building that later served as a Catholic church and in 2004 is the meeting-place of the Loyal Order of Moose. The chapel opened in 1816, but the Sunday school remained at the Dean Street premises until about 1850.

The cost of building this chapel was to be a burden upon Crediton Methodists for many years, and in 1831 there was a proposal to sell it to relieve the debt, but no buyer could be found. However, by 1846 matters must have improved because Crediton was thought worthy of being the head of a new circuit which included many of the surrounding villages. The 1851 religious census indicated that 130 persons worshipped at the Crediton chapel with an attendance of 90 at the Sunday school. The seating capacity was shown as 275.

It was around this time that William Perkins

Harper emerged to become a major benefactor to the church. He had the vision of a 'beautiful new chapel' and saved the money for the purchase of the land. He died in 1880 but the money he left was invested wisely, and in 1891 it amounted to close to £400, which was sufficient to purchase the site in Union Road. In 1892 work was completed on the building which still stands on that site in 2004 and which has been continually used for worship for well over 100 years. The building has been extended and improved on a number of occasions, the last being in 1997 with the erection of a new porch. This work was commissioned to celebrate the centenary of the opening of the building.

Although we are discussing Wesleyan Methodism, mention should also be made of the Bible Christians who had two places of worship in the town. The High Street chapel (now used for a children's playgroup) opened in 1860, and a smaller one at Fordton in 1899. The High Street chapel was extended in 1891, resulting in a number of cottages in Kiddicot being demolished.

The Bible Christians merged with the Wesleyans in 1954. The High Street chapel was taken over by the Brethren, but worship continued at the Fordton chapel until 1967. This chapel became a Post Office and shop for some years, but is now a private residence. Since the closure of the Fordton chapel, Methodism has centred upon the chapel in Union Road.

*The old Unitarian and Congregational meeting-house, later the Sunday school. This building once stood to the rear of Nos. 107 and 108 High Street.* (MRS W. DAVEY)

'A Full House'. The congregation at the opening of the Wesleyan Methodist Church, 1892.

(KEN SAUNDERS, PHOTO BERRY)

Above: The members gather, in 1992, to celebrate the centenary of the opening of the Methodist Church. (KEN SAUNDERS)

Right: Crediton Moose Hall, built in 1816 as a Wesleyan Methodist Chapel. From the end of the First World War until 1969 it was the Roman Catholic Church. After the new church in Park Street was opened the building was deconsecrated and became the meeting rooms of the Loyal Order of Moose.

*Testing the water. For many years Crediton was supplied by water from a reservoir at Walsons near Bow. Every year the Urban District Council would undertake a ceremonial visit to the site to test the quality of the water.*
(A. H. KING ROBINSON)

*Dennis Brinicombe drives his horses through the town in September 2000 in a protest against high fuel prices.*
(CAHMS)

# Chapter 5

# 'Kirton was a Market Town'

## The Market

The first reference to a market in Crediton was that granted by Henry III in 1230, which means that a market was held in the town for over 700 years. Henry also granted a fair to be held on St Lawrence's day, which is 10 August. This fair has been lost but was certainly still in existence in 1743 when the great fire struck the town. In 1309, under a grant from Edward II, the market day was changed from Thursday to Tuesday and two further fairs were granted, on 25 April and 8 September.

In the early-nineteenth century market day was on a Saturday, but this was changed to a Thursday by James Wentworth Buller as part of the Crediton Improvement Act. Within living memory the market was always held on a Tuesday. The last market held in Crediton was on 13 March 1962; the last auction being conducted by 62-year-old Sam Bassett who had handled sales there for 40 years. According to the Urban District Council (UDC) the closure was 'for economy reasons', because, since the Second World War, there had been a switch to larger markets such as Exeter.

The main market of the year was the April 'Great Market'. This was held in the High Street and may well have been a direct continuation of the market granted by Edward II in 1309. The High Street was closed to all traffic and cattle pens were set up in the street. At its peak the market stretched from the Green down as far as where the War Memorial now stands. This was not just a cattle market, however,

*April Great Market. In the background you can see Lane & Son, ladies' outfitters. In 2004 HSBC Bank stands where Lane's shop used to be. (A.H. King Robinson, Photo Berry)*

*April Great Market, c.1910. Cattle overspilling from the High Street into Union Road and possibly beyond. (CAHMS, Miss S. Lewis Collection)*

as there were also stalls selling local produce. Cheapjacks and medicine men also came to sell their goods.

The 1891 census, which was conducted in April, records a number of caravans parked on the Green, presumably for the Great Market. These include the caravan of a Mr James Chipperfield, a showman. Also, there was the caravan of a Mr A. Jones, who was a licensed hawker. He had 12 children, ten of whom were under 16 years of age, all apparently living in one caravan (a definite case of overcrowding).

Mr Les Berry, one of our older citizens and the son of the man who took many of the early photographs reproduced in this book, remembers that there was also a parade of horses, all kitted out in fine brasses, which took place at the end of the auction. The horses were led up Market Street and back down North Street. At the beginning of the twentieth century there was also a fair in the High Street but this was moved to Lord's Meadow in later years.

The last April Great Market in the High Street was probably held in 1951, because on 30 January that year the UDC agreed to save the market for one further year. It continued in name until 1962, but as it was held using the same pens as those used every other week of the year, it must have been a mere shadow of its former self.

The market buildings constructed in the 1830s were kept in use until the early 1950s. Ernest Vigurs, who came to the town in 1922, remembered that the market was already in decline by that time, and

the Pannier Market was closed. His memories of the market buildings were that:

*About half an acre was enclosed by a brick wall. Entrance was by an arched brick building with offices each side of iron gates. The yard was paved with cobblestones and the cattle and sheep pens were in use until the early 1950s.*

When Mr Charles Way bought the Market House Inn he also purchased the market property and used it to garage his coaches. By this time the livestock market had moved to the area which is a car park in 2004. The pens for sheep and cattle were on opposite sides of the market, but, as Les Ashplant recalls, the pigs were sold from carts parked in the market.

*Crediton High Street, early 1900s. Gimblett's Economic Shoe Works is in the left-hand corner, and the right-hand side of the High Street is still culverted. (CAHMS)*

Hooper's Stores, 28 High Street, as it looked in 1923. William Hooper kept this shop from the 1890s until the early years of the twentieth century.

A crowded market-place on a Thursday, early-twentieth century. (MRS W. DAVEY)

The market-place. The photograph was taken on Coronation Day, 1911.

(MRS W. DAVEY)

# How the market area used to look

*The gates to the old market. They stood in Parliament Street, almost directly opposite the entrance to the Three Little Pigs. (BABS STUTCHBURY)*

*One of the corner 'towers' of the old market, on the junction of Market Street and Parliament Street. (BABS STUTCHBURY)*

*Miss Savage's shop at the bottom of Market Street opposite the Council Offices.*
*(BABS STUTCHBURY)*

# The last market at Crediton

*The last market at Crediton on 13 March 1962.*
(ALL THREE IMAGES – BABS STUTCHBURY, PHOTO CHARLES LUXTON)

# The Town

The earliest 'plan' of the town is the Norden Terrier of 1598 which, although it shows the streets, does not provide names for any of them. The Terrier shows that the West Town consisted of the High Street with only one street leading off it, which was North Street. Over the centuries the names of these streets have changed. In the 1740s North Street was called the Back Lane and at another time Litterburn Lane, after the Litterburn which it forded. The High Street itself had three names – at the eastern end it was called St David's Street; the main part, from about North Street to where St Saviours Way is in 2004 was Broad Street; and from there to the Green it was known as Narrow Street. Broad Street was where the market was held prior to it being moved in the 1830s. The Shambles (as the market buildings were called) were situated in the middle of the road and stretched from the top of North Street to Narrow Street. There was a 'pig pen' sited at the eastern end of St Lawrence Green, well away from the other market buildings. Broad Street and Narrow Street are names that survived until the middle of the nineteenth century but the name St David's Street seems to have fallen out of use several years earlier.

At the time the Terrier was drawn up St Lawrence Green was completely surrounded by houses. It was almost certainly not a very salubrious place then as it was probably used for such activities as cock fighting and bear baiting. Also, the St Lawrence Fair was held here over three days starting on 10 August, and this was said to often be a drunken and riotous affair.

Three roads went out from the Green to the west: Back Lane which roughly took the line of Western Road; Lower Road which in later years was called Threshers Causeway and now shortened to just Threshers, and which was probably the main road to the west in those times; and the road leading to Westwood. The Improvement Commissioners Map of 1836 shows a road called Turnagain Lane which is now Alexandra Road. The reason for its name is because the road comes to a dead end.

Further roads were built off the High Street during the nineteenth century. The first was Market Street which was constructed in the 1830s. In the 1860s the Searle Street development was started. This was a sort of suburbia, with local businessmen and the independently wealthy moving there. The houses they built, such as Park Villa and Rose Hill Villa, are still there in 2004. In the latter years of the nineteenth century William Searle, a chemist who was in partnership with Ernest Jackson, and was

probably the Searle after whom the development was named, was one resident; Harry Elston, one of the shoe-factory owners, was another, and he lived at Belmont. At the beginning of the twentieth century the Constitutional (Conservative) Club was opened, and building had started in Peoples Park Road.

*Baptist Chapel Court, in a photograph which was probably taken shortly before it was demolished, mid-twentieth century. (*PHOTO AUTHERS*)*

There have always been many courts and terraces off the High Street. Most have disappeared today, but the names may still be remembered by some Kirtonians. On the south side of High Street, flats have been constructed where Baptist Chapel Court once stood at the foot of the lane leading up to Barnfield; Fountain Court still stands at the time of writing between Nos. 4 and 5, but most of the cottages have gone; Albert Terrace ran back between Nos. 37 and 38; part of St Saviours Court still remains, but before the road was built up to the car park there were at least a dozen cottages in the Court; and Stones Court once stood behind Nos. 65 and 66. Duke Court, behind the Duke of York Inn, is still occupied. On the north side of the High Street, Bell Court still remains; Buckingham Place once stood behind No. 102;

Porch Court still exists and now leads through to Waresfoot Drive, but the cottages have long disappeared; Stanbury Court is now a modern development, but in the past must have been a rabbit warren of small cottages; the entrance to Mann's Court still exists alongside No. 126, but the cottages have gone and the entrance to Bank Place is still there beside the National Westminster Bank.

*Mr and Mrs Smith, both over 90 years old. The photograph was taken in Fountain Court, c.1915. (CAHMS)*

Paradise, a group of 17 two-up two-down cottages, was once near St Lawrence Green, but any cottages that were still standing were demolished to make way for the ambulance station in the late 1960s. In the nineteenth century it must have been a very overcrowded place with, at one time, 92 persons living there – almost half of them were children under 14 years of age. The worst overcrowding was in the cottage of William Passmore who lived in four rooms with his wife and ten children.

The development of the East Town was a little more complicated. This was the site of the original settlement in Creedy and where the roads from both Exeter and Tiverton enter the town. The Norden Terrier shows roads entering from many sources. The most southerly is from the Fordton area passing the Three Mills (clearly the fourth mill was not built until a later century). This road as far as the junction with East Street was known as Mill Street for many years. The northern end of what is now Mill Street was called Bladderstone or Bladderstone Road until the 1860s.

Two roads join Mill Street from the direction of Downes. The first is the present main road from Exeter, but the other joins at the top of White Hart Hill, arriving apparently from over the top of Downes Head, or Wares Downes as it would then have been called. The ancient route to Exeter may well have run over the top of Downes Head.

*St Saviours Court. (CHARLES LUXTON COLLECTION)*

Two further roads join Mill Street at the junction with East Street, one coming from the direction of Downes Head and Commonmarsh Lane past where the town's cider factory once stood, and the other lower one from Lord's Meadow. The area through which these roads approached is called Tolleys. In 2004 it is an area with just a few houses, but in times past it was almost certainly one of the most overcrowded areas in the town. In the mid-nineteenth century there were some 150 people living in 32 houses. A number of these were farm workers on the Buller estate. A Mr Samuel Manning, of independent means, who was certainly not an estate hand, also lived in this area and it is he whom Mannings is named after. This part of the town is thought to have been where St Boniface was born.

At the north end of Bladderstone, Bramble Lane joined the main road. At the time of writing this is the main road to Tiverton, but in times past it is likely to have been a dead end, or too narrow to carry any form of traffic. The name of this road was changed to Exhibition Road in the 1860s after the Devon County Show was held on the site of the school sports ground, known as Exhibition Field. In the past 40 years there has been considerable development in this area of the town with the growth of a substantial trading estate. This has brought many new businesses to the town, and a number of traditional companies have moved there from more central locations.

The name Blagdon is fairly recent and is named after the Blagdon family who built and lived in Blagdon House at the junction of Mill Street and Exhibition Road. Old Tiverton Road was clearly what it states to be, the road to Tiverton before Exhibition Road was made fit for traffic.

On the 1598 map the roads approaching the town from the north are very much as they are in 2004. Pounds Hill was the road to Long Barn, Jockey Hill led to Sandford and North Devon as well as being the main route to Okehampton and on to Cornwall. Deep Lane was the link from the West Town to Jockey Hill.

The central area of the East Town has changed considerably over the centuries, although the street plan is little changed; that is, apart from Charlotte Street, which was constructed in 1836 by James Wentworth Buller and named after his wife.

Dean Street is probably the oldest street in the town and contains some of the oldest surviving buildings. Pevsner suggested that the continuous row of cottages on the west side of the street are much older than their nineteenth-century frontages. Indeed, recently uncovered wooden panelling in one

of the cottages confirms this, as does evidence of what appear to once have been connecting doors between some of the cottages.

Bowden Hill looks very different in 2004 to the way it did even 40 years ago. The flats on the left-hand side replaced a continuous line of cottages. In the nineteenth century and before this must have been a warren of alleys and courtyards. Excluding the Parish Church, the oldest surviving buildings in the town are the Spurway's Almshouses in Park Street, which were built using money bequeathed by Humphrey Spurway who died in 1555.

Brian Little, writing not long after the Second World War, said that the town could not be seen as you approached on the Exeter Road, and that you came upon it suddenly when you reached the station and Taw Vale. This certainly no longer applies, as the houses on Spruce Park and Butt Parks can be seen from as far away as Codshead Bridge.

The twentieth century has seen considerable development. The town has grown up both sides of the valley, and there is very little space left for growth, other than outwards. The fields on the edge of town, which for generations were play areas for children, are now all covered in houses.

*St Lawrence Green, c.1880. The houses in the background are part of an area once known as Paradise, which was renamed St Lawrence Terrace in the 1930s. (CAHMS)*

*Peoples Park, formerly called Buller Park, and prior to that the Rack Field. This is where the kersies would be laid out to dry before being sent to market, probably at Exeter. The first properties to be built on Peoples Park Road were constructed in the early years of the twentieth century. Note the two boys rolling hoops along the road.*
(CAHMS, Margaret Ash, Collection)

*The fountain, East Street. Erected in 1887 to celebrate Queen Victoria's golden jubilee, it was opened by Lady Audrey Buller and consisted of two large horse troughs and a hand-operated spout from which people could drink. It was damaged beyond repair by a car in the 1950s or '60s. (CAHMS)*

*Edwin Tucker's advert – Town Guide 1955. Edwin Tucker & Sons operated from The Maltings at the foot of Jockey Hill. The company was owned by Maurice Webber and their offices were the former Horse and Jockey Inn. In 2004 Tuckers run a country store in Commercial Road. The Maltings in Ashburton are still in operation. (CAHMS)*

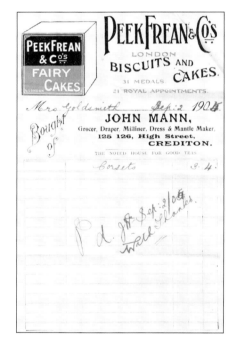

Above: *Invoice from John Mann – Tailor.*
(CAHMS)

Left: *Crediton Crisp Company headed notepaper.*
*The Crediton Crisp Company traded in the 1950s*
*from premises in the yard of the Crediton Inn.*
(CAHMS)

# Traders

Many of the names on and around the High Street have traded in the town for generations. Unfortunately some of these may have been lost in recent years, but they are fondly remembered by the people of the town. The following is by no means a comprehensive list of those past and present, but hopefully covers most of the long-established businesses in the town.

## Cox's

James Cox and his family moved from Morchard Bishop in the 1870s and opened a butcher's shop at 8 Market Street. Unfortunately, James died at the young age of 47, but his widow Louisa carried on the business. In 1894 she moved to 16 High Street where the company has traded from ever since. Louisa died in 1907 and her son Albert took over the business. Albert died childless and the business then passed on to two nephews, Ned Cox and Wilfred Southcott. Ned retired in 1960 and Wilfred in 1975. The business was then sold to an employee, Peter Browning, who ran it until 1998. He sold it to the owner at the time of writing, Mr Eakers.

Back in 1911 Cox's fell foul of a local bylaw which forbade the sale of meat from a premises other than the market-place on a Saturday (market day). The defendants were taken to court by the lord of the manor, Mr Tremayne Buller, found guilty and fined £20. The chairman of the magistrates refused permission to appeal to a higher court.

## A.E. Lee

Clothes have been sold at 17 High Street since the 1870s. The first name to appear in the census was a Mr William Couldred who described himself as a draper and grocer, and later in the century an outfitters was run by Mr Charles Kiell. In 1915 Mr A.E. Lee took over the business and it has been in the Lee family ever since. The proprietor at the time of writing, Mr Simon Lee, who took over in 1993, is the third generation of the family to run the business from No. 17.

The first Mr Lee served his apprenticeship in London before moving to Exeter and then to Crediton. His son, Mr A.C. Lee, took over the business in 1946 because of his father's failing health.

The frontage of the shop has changed little in over a century and is unlikely to do so in the future as the building has been listed. Until there was a serious fire in 1965 the same could be said of the interior.

Many people have commented that going into Lee's used to be like stepping back in time, and even today, much of the old furniture and fittings remain to give an impression of what High Street shopping was once like. With the closure of Summerwell's in 2003, Lee's is now the only gent's outfitters in Crediton.

## Phillips (Printers and Stationers) Ltd

The firm of Phillips & Co. started trading in the 1930s on the site of the former Seven Stars public house. When Horace Turner took it over in 1958 it was just a small shop, with three employees; Jim Narracott, Miss Madge and Ron Avery who lived above the premises. In 1960 they took over Barnes & Co. and shortly after that moved their printing works across the High Street to No. 115. The former skittle alley and gardens were converted to make the additional space for the printing machines.

Horace's son Ken, along with his wife Tina, took over the business in 1975. It was at this time that the company was employing around 12 people, but due to the computerisation of the printing process this number has been gradually reduced.

In 2004 Ken and Tina's son Glenn works in the business, the third generation of the family to do so.

## Helmores

Helmores claim to be probably the oldest established firm of estate agents and valuers in the country, having been in business for over 300 years. The company was founded by William Helmore in 1699 when he handled the transaction of four properties near Exeter. It established a business that was handed down from father to son for the next three centuries. The company moved to Crediton some 120 years ago.

One of the more famous Helmores was Frederick John who was well known for his practical jokes. One the best-known stories about him is when he was being transported from the station to town in Frank Bourne's hansom cab. It is said that Frank would often fall asleep at the reins, but as the horse knew the road from the station it would carry on under its own steam. On one journey Frederick Helmore, realising that Frank had nodded off, jumped out of the cab at the top of White Hart Hill, ran along Park Street, then along Dean Street, and up Union Street to where the offices were then located. Some minutes later Frank arrived only to find Helmore standing in the doorway of his offices. The amazed Frank Bourne is reported to have said. 'It can't be you, maister. You'm be in me cab!'.

*Dick Adams outside his shop in 1950. The business was founded by Harry Adams, also known as Dick, at 123 High Street. It was moved to 120 and later expanded into the neighbouring properties of 119 and 121 High Street. In 2004 the business is run by Dick's two sons, Richard and David. (CAHMS, PHOTO AUTHERS)*

Another of his stories was that of a bull in a china shop. In the early 1900s a bull escaped from one of the pens in the High Street during April Great Market and somehow got into Mr Martin's china shop at No. 144 High Street. According to Mr Helmore the bull was recovered from the shop without a single piece of crockery being damaged!

Frederick's son Herbert (Bert) was the last Helmore to run the company, and is still remembered in the town for his auctions. Bert had no sons to take over the business and when he died 1965 it passed to his partner, Alan Stoyle senr. Alan retained the Helmore name and continued to run the business until 1975, when his two sons John and Alan junr took over. In 1990, Alan's son Rob joined the company, introducing a third generation of Stoyles to continue the Helmore name.

## MOORE BROTHERS

John and George Moore started in the cycle business shortly after the First World War. They ran a shop from Mill Street during most of the 1920s, before graduating to motor cycles and then cars. Having outgrown their Mill Street premises they first moved to 32 High Street, next door to the White Swan, and later a little further up the street to Bank House where they built their garage with the clock above, which became one of the most familiar features of the town centre. The old-style petrol pumps with arms that swung out over the pavement remained in use until the latter years of the twentieth century.

In 2000 the premises were demolished and housing has been constructed on the hillside behind.

*Frederick Helmore conducting an auction at April Great Market, 1880. (ALAN STOYLE)*

*Mitchell's bakery shop front just prior to closure in August 2000. The first baker recorded at 94 High Street was Charles Newbury in 1871. John Mitchell, the grandfather of the last owner, took over the business in 1885 and it remained in the family until it closed. It was originally a small shop, but when the Brethren Chapel closed the bakery business was expanded into that property.* (MARGARET SPRY)

*Bill Mitchell at work in 2000. Bill took over from his father Frederick and ran the company for over 40 years before retiring at the age of 70.* (MARGARET SPRY)

The site where the showroom and petrol pumps once stood is a mini supermarket at the time of writing. Moore Brothers continue to operate on the Lord's Meadow Trading Estate.

## VENN'S

Roy and Muriel Venn started their 'electrical' business in May 1927 around the same time as electric street lights were being installed in the town. Their first premises were in East Street, but the business was soon moved to the site in the High Street, where it remains in 2004. A significant part of their early business involved delivering charged accumulators and Calor gas to the surrounding farms and villages who did not yet have a mains supply.

Roy died in 1940 and Muriel later married Chris Warman. They continued to run the business until they retired in 1973. Clive Jones took over and has run the shop ever since, still trading under the Venn name.

Below: *The inside of Todd's draper's shop.* (BABS STUTCHBURY)

## TODD'S

When Todd's closed in August 1993 the *Crediton Country Courier* described it as the 'end of an era', which indeed it was. There had been a draper's shop at either 117 or 118 High Street ever since the middle of the nineteenth century. The first record of a drapery was in the 1871 census, when Mr Thomas Johns ran a business from No. 118. Ten years later the business was under the name of John Venn who remained there until 1923, but at some point the shop moved from 118 High Street to 117. The next owners were called Cross and they remained at No. 117 until the Todd family arrived in the town in 1950.

The lack of a ladies' outfitters in Crediton is still lamented by many women of the town, especially those who would prefer not to travel into Exeter to purchase items of clothing.

An interesting item in the newspaper report on the closure relates to the fact that the large store-room at the back of the premises was used as a drill hall during the First World War and that there is evidence of a bricked-up doorway connecting 117 and 118, perhaps indicating that they once formed a single property.

*Crediton Co-op was in East Street opposite the church, 1950s or early 1960s. The grocery was where, until 2003, Wenmouth's radio and TV shop stood, and the butchers is a vets' surgery in 2004. The dividend was 6d. (2½p) for every pound spent. The manager was Don Lashbrooke and the 'first hand' Fred West. The names of the ladies in the photo are not known. A Mr Burrows also worked there and lived above the butcher's shop. He also operated a mobile shop which covered surrounding villages as far afield as Bow and Morchard Bishop. (CAHMS, DON LASHBROOKE)*

*Mills Brothers at the corner of North Street and High Street, early in the twentieth century. The premises were formerly owned by Smallridge & Down and there was a foundry at the rear. (CAHMS).*

*Ivor Coram outside his first shoe shop in North Street, 1951.  (IVOR CORAM)*

*Bill Cherry outside Cherry & Symes garage in Union Road in February 1982.  The old petrol pumps can be seen on the left-hand side.  In 1950 they dispensed Regent petrol.  (CREDITON COUNTRY COURIER)*

53

*The High Street in the 1950s, before the need for yellow lines.* (CAHMS)

*John Osborne outside his shop in the High Street in the early 1950s.* (CAHMS)

## Crediton Public Rooms (or Town Hall)

The Town Hall has had a rather chequered history. It originated from the Mechanics Institute or Literary Society which was founded in 1832. This Society did not prosper and so in 1850 a group of the local gentry formed a company called the Crediton Public Rooms Company. The purpose of the company was to provide a hall for entertainment and meetings. Building started in 1852 and the foundation-stone was laid by James Wentworth Buller. No trace of this stone can be found in the building.

The premises were regularly used for concerts, public meetings and lectures over the next 40 years, but it gradually fell into disrepair and was eventually closed to the public in 1891. It was hoped that the newly formed Crediton Urban District Council would purchase the building for the town, but this did not happen. The company that had formed in 1850 went into liquidation, a new company was formed, and money was raised to repair the building.

The rear of the building for many years housed the fire-engine. Later, this part was leased to the Constitutional Club, who later bought it. In the 1920s the hall was used as the Crediton Electric Cinema, showing films three nights a week with a Saturday matinee for children. During both world wars it was taken over by the military.

Later the British Legion took over the property and the Public Rooms Company was wound up. For many years after the Second World War it was used for shows, dances, parties and dinners; many older Kirtonians will have fond memories of those events. In the 1960s the front section of the hall was sold to a private buyer and for many years was used as a furniture store.

In the 1990s the hall came back into public hands having been purchased by the Crediton Development Trust. At the time of writing the Tourist Information Centre is housed on the ground floor, but there are extensive plans to renovate the property and restore it to how it looked when it was initially constructed. It is hoped that by the time you read this the work will have been completed and the 'Town Hall' will once again be a facility that is used by, and exists for the benefit of, the people of the town.

## The Crediton Workhouse

The Poor Law Act of 1834 introduced the concept of the local board or 'Union', which was a move away from the parish to government. Prior to this the welfare of the poor had been the responsibility of the parish, and standards varied widely from place to place. The new law introduced the concept of the workhouse, where a pauper would be given a roof over his or her head and a basic diet in return for enforced labour. This was certainly not intended to be a soft option as the regime was hard and facilities very basic. It was intended as a disincentive to register as a pauper. Under this Act a person could no longer live outside the workhouse and be in receipt of aid.

Crediton had had a workhouse since the seventeenth century, situated in a building behind the Parish Church, but this was demolished in 1838. A new workhouse was built at around the same time at Threshers on the extreme western end of the town, and by 1841 it had 119 registered inmates. The first master was William Leach who remained in charge until the 1860s. The building was large enough to accommodate just under 200 people.

The severity of the regime very much depended on the master, and there are many horror stories of life in workhouses. However, no such stories survive about Crediton, so perhaps we can assume things were not too harsh. Indeed, towards the end of the century a schoolmistress was provided for the education of the children of the residents.

There was a severe depression in the agricultural industry during the 1850s. This, together with the falling off of the wool trade, meant that times must have been hard for the townspeople. The 1851 census bears this out with 187 inmates at the workhouse, but a further 137 persons on parish relief 'outside'. This situation was against the law at the time, but with the potential of such overcrowding the authorities were left with no choice.

Numbers in the workhouse fell away over the following years to a situation where, in 1901, there were 85 residents, which included two vagrants. Vagrants were often allowed a bed and a meal at the workhouse in return for a few hours' labour, usually gardening or other work on the grounds.

If a girl 'got into trouble' in those days she would most likely have gone into the workhouse to have her baby and, unless she was fortunate enough to find someone to employ her or had a very understanding family, she may well have remained there for some time.

The number of inmates continued to fall in the twentieth century until 1931 when, at 89, numbers had increased back to the levels of the turn of the century; presumably a reflection of the depression of that decade. These are the last records available as by the time of the 1951 census the building had ceased to function as a workhouse. By that time the Crediton building was in use as an institution for the 'mentally deficient', as it was so quaintly put in those days. In fact, until the arrival of care in the community in the 1980s, around 100 women lived there in a controlled environment. In 2004 the former workhouse building consists of luxury flats.

## Bread Riots

*Church Street in the 1950s. (PHOTO AUTHERS)*

Although the town had prospered due to the wool trade for many centuries, there were times of hardship, especially from the late-eighteenth century when that trade had started to die off.

The first reported incident of rioting was on Monday 13 April 1795 following cuts in the parish poor-relief rate. James Buller rode in from Downes to read the Riot Act. Most of the men in the crowd dispersed but the women remained shouting, 'words won't feed our families.' The army was called from Exeter and two of the women were arrested. They were both sentenced to a week in gaol and a whipping.

Trouble also occurred during the agricultural depression of the middle years of the nineteenth century. In May 1847 rioting broke out in the Bowden Hill area of the town. The crowd consisted of mainly women and children who made their way up through Broad Street and on to the Green, smashing shop windows as they went. It was swelled by unemployed navvies who were in the area looking for work on the railway. James Wentworth Buller dealt with the matter locally on this occasion by swearing in over 200 special constables. The rioters were dispersed in the early evening.

This was not the end of the trouble, however, for at around midnight a crowd attacked Mr John Wippell's shop in Church Street. He repelled the mob by throwing his bread at them from an upstairs window. The constables were still in the town on the following morning but the crowds dispersed peacefully.

The riots of January 1854 were reported in full in both the *Western Times* and the *Exeter Flying Post*. The winter of 1853/4 had been a particularly severe one; the *Western Times* reported that 'the weather continues intensely cold, the snow has continued falling for the last three or four days and in some places is many feet deep.'

The troubles started on the evening of Friday 6 January, with snow still lying on the ground. All through the day there had been a large group of people (mainly women) parading the streets begging, and apparently the more fortunate people of the town had been quite generous. Also, in common with the situation seven years earlier, there were a number of navvies employed on the construction of the North Devon Railway in the town who were unable to work, and therefore earn any money, because of the bad weather.

This time the disturbances started on the Green where a relatively small group had assembled amidst rumours that the bakers had increased the price of bread. It started with the group throwing snowballs, but as the numbers of the crowd began to grow the situation became more violent. They first attacked the shops of Mr Thomas Hodge and Mrs Charlotte Herring, breaking the windows of both premises. They then moved on to Mr Simon Lee's shop at the top end of the High Street where the worst scenes of violence seem to have occurred. The newspaper account suggests that the mob partially demolished the building, breaking every pane of glass in the front of the house and the partition between the shop and the kitchen. They also destroyed gas lights and took away around 150 loaves of bread.

The rioters continued to move down the High Street, but by this time the local tradesmen had managed to organise themselves and the few constables that had been sworn in had arrested two persons. Damage was restricted in this area because the owners had 'shuttered up' their premises. However, it was reported that a local butcher, Mr Nickels, had suffered cuts to the head from stones and other missiles thrown by the mob.

It seems that by this time the crowd had started to split up. Some went down North Street and into Parliament Street where they damaged the shop of Mr George Gribble. Another group went into Church Street where Mr John Wippell's shop was attacked. A third group carried on down East Street where they attacked a shop owned by Mr Pinson. They also went on to Mr William Lee's shop, but finding it shuttered up they attacked his private residence next door smashing over 30 panes of glass.

This seems to have been the end of the violence for the evening, but on the following morning a large mob assembled at the market. There was no trouble on that day but, in view of the events of the previous evening, many traders declined to open for business that morning. Of the two men who had been arrested, Mr Richard Burgoyne was discharged with an admonition due to a lack of evidence against him, and Mr John Hubber was committed to the county gaol to await trial there.

These events highlighted the need for a proper police force in the town. Many other towns in Devon had by this time got their own police forces, but not Crediton. However, within a few years a local force had been appointed and a police station built at the bottom of Market Street (the Council Offices in 2004).

## A Public Hanging

As far as is known only one public hanging ever took place in Crediton. This occurred in 1685 when Thomas Hobbs was hanged, probably at the Green, for his part in the Monmouth Rebellion.

## The Crediton Improvement Act, 1836

The *Yeovil Mercury* of 15 July 1836 reported that at a celebration dinner held at Williams' Ship Inn to commemorate the passing of the Act, Mr James Wentworth Buller said in reference to the reputation of the town of Crediton that:

*he thought it a truly important object that the stigma that had so long hung over it should be removed. This bill then was a means whereby nuisances and grievances could be removed. They would all see the benefit to be derived, and he trusted that the town of Crediton would really become one town, and not as it surely was at present, merely a straggling connection of towns.*

These few words say a great deal about what Crediton must have been like at the beginning of the nineteenth century. The town was clearly run down, probably due to the decline of the cloth industry, and as yet there was little to replace it. Also, it seems that the town was dirty and road communication poor. The Improvement Act provided for a number of things including the paving, cleansing, lighting and watching of the streets, lanes and entries; and for the removal of 'various nuisances'.

Prior to the passing of the Act the only means of moving between the East and West Towns was either by a lengthy detour along Mill Street (or

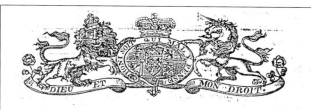

ANNO SEXTO

# GULIELMI IV. REGIS.

### Cap. XXV.

An Act for paving, lighting, watching, cleansing, and otherwise improving the Town of *Crediton* in the County of *Devon*.    [19th May 1836.]

WHEREAS the Town of *Crediton* in the County of *Devon* is an ancient Town, and large and populous, and a Place of considerable Thoroughfare, and the several Streets, Lanes, Entries, and other public Passages and Places within the same are not sufficiently paved, cleansed, lighted, or watched, and are subject to various Nuisances and other public. Inconveniences: And whereas *James Wentworth Buller* Esquire claims to be the Lord of the Manor of *Crediton*, with the Rights, Members, and Appurtenances thereof, and to be entitled to the Customs, Tolls, and Duties of and arising from the Fairs and Markets held within the same Town: And whereas it would tend greatly to the Safety, Convenience, and Advantage, not only of the Inhabitants of the said Town and Neighbourhood, but to all Persons resorting to and travelling through the same, if the said Streets, Lanes, Entries, and other public Passages and Places were properly paved, lighted, watched, cleansed, widened, and improved, and nearer and better Approaches to the said Town were made, under the Authority of Commissioners to be appointed for that Purpose; and if some of the said Streets, Lanes, Entries, public Passages or Places were stopped up, altered, or diverted, and other public Streets, Roads, and Passages opened and made, and certain Buildings used as Butchers Shambles and other Buildings in the chief Street of the said Town were taken down, and if all Obstructions, Nuisances, and Annoyances therein were totally removed and in future prevented; but such beneficial Purposes

[*Local.*]                7 E                poses

(CREDITON TOWN COUNCIL)

Bladderstone as the northern end was known then), up Blagdon, along Belle Parade and up North Street; or by climbing over the top of Bowden Hill. The construction of Union Street made this journey simple and joined up the two distinct halves of the town into the one town that we know today.

The High Street was also improved and widened. At that time the lower part of the High Street was known as Broad Street and the part approaching the Green, Narrow Street. The market was situated in Broad Street with 'The Shambles', which consisted of animal pens and shops, in the middle of the road. As part of the improvements a new market-place was constructed at the bottom of the new Market Street. The Shambles was demolished, thus making the passage of traffic through Broad Street much easier. Although the market was moved to Market Street in the 1830s, the annual April Great Market was still held in the High Street until the middle of the twentieth century. Narrow Street was also widened and the 'pig pens' removed. The Back Lane (now Western Road) through to Barnstaple Cross was also widened.

By the middle of the nineteenth century the High Street would have looked quite similar to the way it does in 2004 but, unlike today, it would have provided an open thoroughfare for traffic to pass easily through the town, and to make use of the services of the High Street traders. Prior to this most through traffic would not have gone into the West Town at all. Travellers to both Barnstaple and Okehampton would have taken the turnpikes along Mill Street, up over Forches Hill and either on to Barnstaple Cross or West Sandford and Newbuildings.

The Act had considerable opposition on its passage through Parliament, mainly from two local landowners – Revd Jonas Dennis and Mr George Yarde. Their objections appear to have arisen from the late inclusion of a proposal for a new road from 'Northernhay' on the Exeter Road to Four Mills (i.e. Station Road), and both men stood to lose land as a result of this proposal. Their objections were rejected by the Parliamentary Committee and this seems to have hardened their opposition to the Act. The two gentlemen also owned a substantial amount of land on Bowden Hill – land which was required for the construction of Union Road. Once the Act was passed they withdrew their consent for the purchase of this land by the commissioners. The land was used to dispose of 'waste' that would otherwise run down into the Litterburn, which at that time flowed through what is Newcombes Meadow in 2004. There was lengthy correspondence over this, but the two men refused to budge.

Under the provisions of the Act disputes were to be resolved by a jury. This jury, which consisted of local landowners who were not of the parish of Crediton, met at the Ship Inn on 31 October 1836. They found in favour of the commissioners and set values of £55 on the land at Four Mills and £252.11s.3d. (£252.56) on the land at Bowden Hill. An early version of compulsory purchase!

The majority of the contracts for the construction of roads were let to Mr Stephen Hatcher of Stoke Canon. The effort required to complete this work must have kept Mr Hatcher in Crediton for some time, for by the 1840s we see him as a resident of the town. Contracts were also let to local builders including William Berry and John Channon. In order to ensure a reasonable standard of work the contractors were required to maintain the roads and other constructions for a period of 12 months after completion.

The commissioners continued to oversee improvements to the town, which included the provision of street lighting and a proper sewerage system, until the end of the nineteenth century. In 1894 the Local Government Act transferred the powers of the commissioners to the Crediton Urban District Council, but the Crediton Improvement Act has never been repealed.

The improvements must have been successful, for the *County Directory* of 1857 reported: 'Crediton... Where the streets are well lighted and paved and wears an air of comfort and respectability seldom met within a town of this size.' The Act is typical of an age where the local nobility took action to 'improve' their cities and towns, but it must be remembered that such improvements were very much dependent on the level of their energy and commitment. Crediton can consider itself lucky that the lord of the manor and other important citizens took such an interest in the prosperity of the town.

*James Wentworth Buller.*
(HENRY PARKER)

# Chapter 6

# Notable Families and Their Homes

## The Lords of the Manor of Crediton

The lordship of the manor of Crediton was for many years invested in the church. In the years the bishop's seat was at Crediton it was the Bishop of Crediton who was the lord of the manor, but when the see moved to Exeter, so did the title. During the Reformation it was briefly given to Sir Thomas Darcy in 1545, but the King, Henry VIII, took it the following year. For the next 50 years the lordship moved between the monarch and the Bishop of Exeter. However, in 1595 Sir William Killigrew bought the title from Gervase Bishop of Exeter. Since then it has been vested in a series of landowning families, including the Ivies and the Strodes. In 1810 Benjamin Cleave of Newcombes became lord of the manor. He was succeeded by James Wentworth Buller, and the title remained with that family until the death of Mowbray Buller in 1948. Since then the title has not been claimed.

## Downes and the Buller Family

Downes was built in 1692 by a prosperous Exeter merchant called Moses Gould, and the house has remained with his descendants to the time of writing. Moses had a son called William who married into the Quicke family of Newton St Cyres. William and his wife Elizabeth had two daughters, Elizabeth, who was heiress to Downes, and Frances. In 1739 Elizabeth married James Buller of Morval, near Looe in Cornwall, and thus the Buller family first came to the Crediton area. Since then several generations of the family have owned the estate, including most notably General Sir Redvers Buller who inherited it in 1874. The owners of Downes at the time of writing are Mr and Mrs Henry Parker who live there with their two children, Redvers and Stroma. The Parkers are direct descendants of the Bullers as Mr Parker's mother Rosemary was the daughter of Mowbray

Buller who owned the house from 1917 to 1948. Mrs Parker was heavily involved in Crediton activities and is fondly remembered in the town. She was responsible for beginning the steam-engine rallies that were held in May (now moved to September) and was involved in the local Red Cross, the Town Band and the History and Museum Society. During the Second World War she drove ambulances in the Hammersmith area of London, transporting Blitz victims.

Downes was described by Pevsner as 'sited on a slight rise with fine views to the south.' It is a two-storey building, built of brick, but since 1794 has been faced with Beer stone. Considerable alterations were made in the nineteenth and early-twentieth centuries. The original entrance was at the front, but in the 1850s was moved to the west side. In 1910 Tremayne Buller made extensive alterations to the east wing and in the late 1970s part of the large service wings at the rear of the building were demolished.

Inside the most notable features are the staircase with an impressive carved ceiling by John Abbot of Frithelstock in North Devon, and the panelled sitting-room. Part of the panelling is dated 1604, which predates the house by some 90 years. It was brought from Dunscombe by the Gould family.

The Buller family have had a significant influence on the town over the years. James Wentworth Buller, whose main achievements are described elsewhere in this book, owned the house from 1827 to 1865. He and his wife Charlotte had nine children, three of whom were to be owners of the house and lords of the manor. Their second son, Redvers, is surely the most famous member of the family, and his life is described later.

In more recent times Dame Georgiana, who was the only child of Sir Redvers and Lady Audrey, is remembered for her pioneering work in hospital administration and in the care and training of the disabled. She first made her mark in the First World War where she was appointed as head of the Exeter VAD (Voluntary Aid Detachment). The role of the VAD was to look after wounded servicemen.

*Redvers Buller as a young man.* (HENRY PARKER)

responsible for more than 1,500 beds. In 1920 she was made a DBE in recognition of her contribution to the VAD service.

After the war she channelled her efforts into local hospital projects. In the 1920s she became chairman of the appeal committee set up to raise money for a polio and TB hospital in Exeter. The hospital was opened by the late Queen Mother who asked that it be named after her newborn daughter Elizabeth. The Princess Elizabeth Hospital remained on the same site until the end of the twentieth century.

Perhaps Miss Buller's most noted achievement, however, was the foundation in 1937 of 'St Loyes College for the Rehabilitation and Training of the Disabled.' At the time of writing the college has an international reputation for the quality of its courses which prepare disabled people for employment in a variety of skills in the outside world. Dame Georgiana died in 1953 at the age of 70.

The last surviving holder of the Buller name in the Crediton area was Miss Millicent, daughter of Tremayne (the younger brother of Sir Redvers) and Elinor Buller. Millicent was born in 1899 and died in 2002. She lived in London for over 20 years following the death of her father in 1948, and spent much of this time working for the Red Cross. She was awarded the MBE for her services to the movement. After she returned to Devon in 1970 she worked as a volunteer steward at Exeter Cathedral. She continued this work until well after her 100th birthday, and could be seen driving into Exeter and back every Wednesday. Indeed she was still driving at the age of 101.

As casualties increased, the War Office took more direct control of the VAD hospitals, but Miss Buller remained the administrator at Exeter, the only woman to hold such a post. At this time she was

*Miss Millicent Buller pictured in 1916 with her pony 'Pat'.* (CAHMS)

# General Sir Redvers Buller, VC

Redvers Buller was almost certainly the most famous Kirtonian of recent times. He was born in 1839, the second son of James Wentworth Buller and his wife Charlotte. As the second son he would not have expected to inherit the family seat, Downes, and he therefore chose a military career; one that would bring him national and international fame. Due to the death of his elder brother, James Howard Buller, at a fairly young age, he did in fact inherit Downes and the title of lord of the manor of Crediton. His military duties did make him something of an absentee landlord until his retirement following the Boer War, but as we shall see he was loved and respected in the town, the county of Devon and far beyond.

His first Army commission was as ensign in the 60th Rifles, later the King's Royal Rifle Corps (the regiment is now the 2nd Battalion the Royal Green Jackets). He spent the majority of his career overseas, with postings to India, China, Canada, the Ashanti (West Africa), South Africa for the Zulu War, the Sudan, Ireland and finally back to South Africa to fight the Boers. Following the Zulu War he returned home and spent a short period on administrative duties mainly in London. During this period he married Lady Audrey Howard, the widow of a cousin whom he had known for a long time. He was 42. The couple had one child – Georgiana.

Buller achieved his greatest fame during the Boer War, but he won his Victoria Cross fighting against the Zulus. The action took place in 1879 on the Hloblane (pronounced Choblane) Mountain where Buller was leading a reconnaissance party. The Zulus were there in numbers and cut off his retreat. Buller first rescued Lieutenant Everett who had had his horse stabbed from under him. He then went back into the fray at least three further times to rescue others when the position had seemed hopeless.

An account of the time describes Buller as:

*... leading his men at a swinging canter, with his reins in his teeth, a revolver in one hand and a knobkerrie snatched from a Zulu in the other, his hat blown off in the melee and a large streak of blood across his face...*

On his return to Devon he received a great welcome with a dinner given in his honour at Exeter Guildhall. In London he was appointed Aide de Camp to Queen Victoria and promoted to colonel. In 1885 he was honoured with a knighthood.

At the outbreak of the Boer War in 1899, at the age of 60, he was offered the post of commander-in-chief of the British forces, an honour he accepted

General Sir Redvers Buller, VC, early in the twentieth century. (HENRY PARKER)

reluctantly. By the time he arrived in South Africa the initial stages of the war had gone badly. Sir George White was surrounded at Ladysmith, and both Mafeking and Kimberley besieged. Buller's first attempt to relieve Ladysmith ended in failure and with heavy loss of life, as did his second attempt which ended in the defeat at Spion Kop. A third attempt was also unsuccessful. On his fourth attempt to relieve White, Buller changed his tactics and concentrated his heavy artillery on Boer positions dug into the hillsides surrounding the town. This time he was successful and the Boers were in retreat. With victory apparently won Buller was sent home to England. However, it would be a further 18 months before the final victory over the Boers was achieved.

The General was given a hero's welcome on his return to England in 1900 – he was presented with the freedom of the city of Exeter, and when he reached Crediton he was welcomed by large cheering crowd. A newspaper report of the time said that on the day of his return the locals 'practically kept the day as a holiday'. The church bells were ringing, the station was bedecked with flags and at the entrance there was a triumphal arch. It is said that the streets were

*Downes decorated for the return of Sir Redvers from the Sudan. The date in the crest above the door is 19 April 1884. (HENRY PARKER)*

*The train carrying General Buller approaches Crediton on his triumphant return from the Boer War on 10 November 1900. (CAHMS)*

decorated from St Lawrence Green to Downes. He was processed through the town, led by mounted police and a military band.

There was some criticism of Buller, mainly in the London press, but the people of Devon recognised him only as a hero. Among many honours, he was presented with an album containing 20,000 greetings from well-wishers. Each subscriber had to pay 6d. (2½p) to have their message included (not an insignificant sum in those days). It speaks much of the respect with which he was held by the people of Devon that so many were prepared to contribute. A further example of the esteem in which he was held

is shown by the 50,000 people from home and abroad who contributed to an appeal to erect a statue in his honour. This statue was unveiled in 1905 and stands outside Exeter College in New North Road, Exeter, and it is engraved with three simple words: 'He saved Natal.'

He retired to Downes soon after his return from South Africa and took up the duties of lord of the manor. General Sir Redvers Buller died in June 1908 at the age of 68 and was buried in Crediton church-yard with full military honours. Crediton's memorial to its famous son is a carved frieze in the eastern wall of the nave of the church.

*Railway staff awaiting the arrival of General Buller's train on his return from the Boer War, 1900.* (HENRY PARKER)

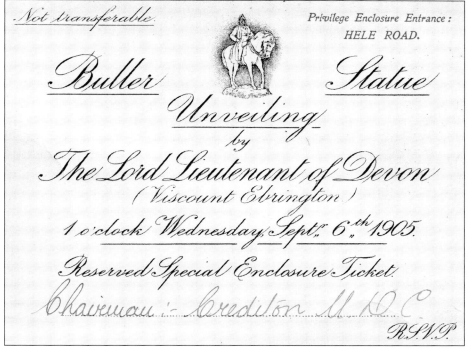

Above: *Soldiers of the Devon Yeomanry (now the Royal Greenjackets) processing behind General Buller's coffin. This photograph also gives a good view of East Street as it looked in 1908.* (SUE BROWN, PHOTO BERRY)

Right: *General Sir Redvers Buller's coffin arriving at Crediton Parish Church, 5 June 1908.* (SUE BROWN, PHOTO BERRY)

Right: *General Buller's horse – you can just pick out the boots reversed in the stir-rups.* (SUE BROWN, PHOTO BERRY)

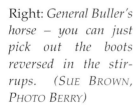

Left: *Floral tributes on General Buller's grave.*
(SUE BROWN, PHOTO BERRY)

## The Davie Family of Creedy Park

The influence of the Davie family, later Ferguson Davie, was mainly on the parish of Sandford, but successive generations were governors of Crediton Parish Church and were involved in the development of the town.

The baronetcy was first conveyed on Sir John Davie who was a physician. It was said that in the nineteenth century Sir Humphrey Davie was very generous to the poor of his parish, so much so that in his time 'there was a rush for cottages in Sandford.' Sir Humphrey had no sons, but when his daughter married Col Ferguson he took the name of Ferguson Davie and a new hereditary baronetcy was conferred.

In 1610 Sir John Davie had almshouses constructed in Church Street for the poor of the parish. These houses were demolished in 1960 and replaced by the present block of flats.

Creedy House was built by William Burn for Col H.R. Ferguson Davie but was destroyed by fire in 1915. Many important documents were lost in this fire, most notable of all was the original of Norden's famous 1598 map of Crediton – fortunately there are several copies in existence. The house was rebuilt between 1916 and 1921 by Dart & Francis for Arthur Ferguson Davie. The estate was broken up in 1975 and the house converted into 13 units in 1982.

Above: *Creedy House before the 1915 fire.  (CAHMS)*

Right: *Construction work in progress to rebuild Creedy House. The work was undertaken by Dart & Francis; this photograph bears the date 22 March 1919.  (CHARLIE GREENSLADE)*

*Creedy House, c.1914. (CAHMS)*

*The Davie Almshouses in Church Street as they were in the early years of the twentieth century.*
*(PHOTO BERRY)*

*Demolishing the Davie Almshouses in Church Street, 1959/60.*

ON THIS SITE, FOR NIGH ON
THREE HUNDRED AND FIFTY YEARS,
STOOD ALMSHOUSES FOR POOR PERSONS
OF SANDFORD AND CREDITON,
PROVIDED BY JOHN DAVIE ESQRE., OF CREEDY
AND MAINTAINED BY HIS DESCENDANTS.
A. D. 1611 ~ 1959.

## Shobrooke Park

Shobrooke Park is a fairly recent name given to an ancient manor. Similarly, the family name Shelley is a relatively new name to be resident at the manor. As with the Creedy estate much of the land is outside of Crediton, but the owners have often had a significant influence on the town.

The original name of the estate was Little Fulford. The first Fulford House was built by Sir William Perriam and later sold to the Tuckfield family. *Risdon's Survey of Devon* (revised in 1811) tells us that the house was rebuilt in 1810 to a design by Hakewill, and the estate remained in the Tuckfield family:

*... until the death of Miss Elizabeth Tuckfield about four years ago [1807], when it descended, under the will of her brother, John Tuckfield, MP for Exeter, to Richard Hippisley, Esq. eldest son of the Rev. John Hippisley, of Stow in the Wold, Gloucestershire, who has taken the name of Tuckfield.*

Little Fulford was an extensive estate in those days, for Risden also records that Mr Richard Hippisley-Tuckfield also owned the manors of Tetburne (Tedburn St Mary) and Posbery (Posbury).

Richard's wife Charlotte was an interesting lady in her own right. She founded an elementary school in the village of Posbury in 1835 – an establishment which was way ahead of its time, because it would be another 50 years before a basic education became compulsory and therefore available to all. However, before she opened this school she had been educating a number of 'deaf and dumb' children at Shobrooke. This enterprise eventually led to the foundation of the Royal West of England School for the Deaf. In 2004 a portrait of Charlotte hangs in the hallway of this establishment.

Sir John Frederick Shelley is the best-remembered owner of Shobrooke in recent times. He died in March 1976 at the age of 92 and is remembered as a governor of the Grammar School and, of course, by the new school built at the top of Barnfield in the 1960s which bore his name. He was member of Crediton Rural District Council for 47 years and served on Devon County Council for 40 years. He was chairman between 1946 and 1955.

Sir John married twice. His first wife, Nora, was the daughter of Mr F.J. Coleridge Boles of Rackenford Manor. They were married in 1912, but she died in 1953. Later that year he married Marianne Mee.

The house was used as a boarding-school during the Second World War, but in 1947 it was destroyed by a fire in which two pupils died. However, the impressive nineteenth-century terraced gardens do remain and are open to the public on selected dates during the year.

*Skating on Shobrooke Pond, January 1933. The man second on the left is Sir John Shelley.*

## Newcombes

The name Newcombe first appeared in 1693 when John Speke sold land in Crediton to a William Newcombe. History does not record what this Mr Newcombe did with the land, other than that he sold it to Robert Stone 30 years later. It was he who built 'The Great House', and 'two other brick dwellings with walled gardens'.

Robert Stone died intestate in 1741 and it was a further 30 years before an Act of Parliament declared his grandson, Robert Cooke, as heir. The Act also ordered him to sell the property to meet the demands of his grandfather's creditors. It was at this time that the property came to the Cleave family and remained with them until the end of the nineteenth century.

John Courtis Skewes, after whom Courtis Gardens is named, owned the property in the early years of the twentieth century, and in 1936, a year before Skewes died, Mr Albert White of the building firm White & Sons bought it. He sold the mansion to Mr Maurice Webber.

*Newcombes House. (CAHMS)*

## The Newcombes Trust

In March 1939 the Gaumont British Picture Corporation Ltd bought the remaining land of the Newcombes estate, and for the duration of the Second World War they used the site to produce films, constructing a number of temporary buildings on what were said to be beautifully laid-out formal gardens. During that time over 100 people lived on the estate, mostly in the recently constructed temporary accommodation. Most of the people living there were technical staff evacuated from London, but a few local people were employed. Among them was Mrs Dora Blackmore (formerly Mrs Blaen) who recalls watching pre-release versions of films in the cinema block. Most of the people of the town had to wait until the films went on general release and reached the Palace Cinema. On a Saturday the cinema was converted into a dance hall, and the people of Crediton were invited to join in. Mrs Blackmore remembers that as there was a shortage of local male dance partners (most of the local men were away on active service) American servicemen were bussed in, probably from barracks at Pinhoe, to even up the numbers. She recalls that the Americans were quite popular with the women of the town, but less so with the remaining male population!

At the cessation of hostilities, and with London no longer under the threat of bombing, Gaumont moved their operations back to the capital. In October 1946 they sold the land to four local men – Richard Roach, Seymour Fell Pope, Frederick Authers and Sir John Frederick Shelley Bart. These men, along with others, soon after formed the Newcombes Trust.

The *Crediton Gazette* of 1 August 1946 carried a report on a public meeting that had been held a few weeks earlier with the purpose of purchasing the site, with the initial objective of providing temporary accommodation to meet the housing shortage in the town. The report quotes Mr Roach as saying that:

*... he had had to go into some of the hovels in Crediton lately, and the conditions were deplorable. 'If we don't do it now, we shall be cursed in Crediton for generations to come.'*

In 2004, a relatively short time after these events, it seems hard to believe that there was a severe shortage of housing for local people, possibly local war heroes, and that some were still living in 'hovels'.

The temporary wooden chalets were to be used to ease the housing shortage in the immediate postwar years, and with the construction of the Spruce Park and Butt Parks housing estates in the 1950s, many of the tenants only remained in them for a few years. However, it was the end of 1963 before the last three tenants, Miss M. Evans, Mr W. Stanbury and Mr L. Evans, moved on. The 'temporary' wooden huts were demolished in 1966.

In October 1960 the huts were put to a good use housing five families who had been made homeless by the Fordton floods. Messrs Lyne, Dyer and Salter, along with Mrs Bell, only remained there for a few months, but Mr Essery did not move out until July 1963. At Christmas 1963 Lennard House opened, providing more modern and comfortable accommodation – it is not known whether the three remaining tenants moved there.

Following the war there was a number of changes to the property. The British Restaurant was closed down in March 1947 and in May part of the first floor and the whole of the second floor of the mansion house was leased to the Ministry of Health for a health centre. In 1971 the Newcombes Housing Association sold part of the land to Devon County Council who had the mansion house demolished to make way for a modern health centre. In 1972 they sold a further part of the estate to the British Legion Housing Association who built the present flats and houses in Lennard Road. The Lodge remained until 1978 before it too was demolished.

The Newcombes Trust is still active at the time of writing, their latest project being new houses in Parliament Street behind the Telephone Exchange.

# Chapter 7

# Industry Past and Present

## Agriculture

From the earliest days of the Saxon settlement right through almost to the time of writing, Crediton has been heavily reliant on farming and its produce, being set in the midst of some of the most fertile and productive farming land in the country. Throughout this time it has been the market town at the centre of an active agricultural industry, yet agriculture has rarely been the main employer of the townspeople.

Over the centuries a succession of cottage- and later factory-based industries have been the main means of employment.

Agriculture and its produce has been the source on which the town has made its wealth in times gone by – indeed at the height of the wool trade Crediton was said to have been one of the 50 most prosperous towns in the country. Most of the raw materials, such as wool for the weaver and animal hides for the tanner to produce leather for the shoemaker, were for

*John Roach with his prize pigs at a showing at Wellparks. The Kyrtonian breed won at shows in the West Country for many years, and in 1961 they swept the board at the Smithfield Show, a feat never achieved before or since. The head pigman at Wellparks in those years was Bill Hannaford of Hookway. (MRS JEAN ROACH, PHOTO AUTHERS)*

centuries provided from local farms, along with meat and produce to feed the townspeople. Indeed, if we look back to why the original settlement by the Creedy grew and prospered, it was due to the quality of the land and its ability to provide sufficient produce to support a monastic community.

Census records show that in 1841 almost 200 persons (more than 10 per cent of the working population) living within the confines of the town were described as agricultural labourers or similar. However, by 1901 this number had dropped to 60. A similar examination of the surrounding villages and hamlets, although showing a fall in the numbers employed due to mechanisation, would not show as significant a drop.

In the early-twenty-first century the links are not as strong as they were, yet milk is still brought in to the processing plant in East Street, and there are still working mills at Fordton that need supplies of grain. Also, High Street traders are still reliant on custom from the surrounding area.

The twentieth century saw the town expand and engulf land that had been farmed for centuries. Westwood Farm is now almost surrounded by the Western Lea development, and at the other end of the town new estates have crept along Exhibition Road to engulf what used to be Blagdon and Bradley Farms. Also, in the 1950s the new council estates of Spruce Park and Butt Parks took much of the land belonging to Park Farm. These are just a few examples – there are many more.

*Albert Place (behind 42 High Street), formerly Hooker's Linhay, showing the Weavers Cottages.*

(MARGARET WOLLACOTT)

*John Roach's Kyrtonian White.* (MRS JEAN ROACH)

## The Wool Industry

The wool industry was the main employer for centuries, the first local record of the trade being in 1301. Indeed from the fourteenth through to the end of the eighteenth century, apart from a brief decline in the mid-fifteenth century, the town grew wealthy and prospered on the production of cloth – in the early days kersies and later serges and flax. The antiquary John Leland, on his travels through England between 1534 and 1543, remarked that there was

'a praty [economically vibrant] Market in Kirton.' 'The Toun usith Clothing, and most hereby lyvith.'

In those times Crediton was famous throughout Europe for the quality of its goods, with large amounts being exported mainly to Holland and Germany, although Portugal was also a significant customer – 'as fine as Kirton spinning' was a phrase widely used to denote quality. Thomas Westcote, writing in 1630, referred to the 'aptness and diligent industry of the inhabitants' which gave it a reputation above all other towns. To prove this he reported the often-repeated story 'that 140 threads of woollen yarn spun in that town were drawn together through the eye of a tailor's needle.' This phenomenon could be viewed for many years in a tailor's shop in Watling Street, London.

The decline of the industry began in the eighteenth century with the arrival of new machinery. The industrial revolution and the growth of factory production methods in the North West and the Midlands brought the end for the industry throughout the South West. Towns like Crediton were unable to cope with the competition, mainly due to the lack of coal to drive the steam-powered machines. The nearest significant coal supply was in South Wales but it was completely uneconomical to transport it to the South West. These powerful machines could produce in one morning more yarn than a dozen people working on hand looms could spin in a week.

The end was gradual, however. There were still several factories in production at the beginning of the nineteenth century, and a cottage industry remained until the last quarter of the century. In 1841 there were still some 280 townspeople working as weavers, but 50 years later in 1891 only three people were claiming to earn a living from the trade. One of the last factories to close in the town was probably that of Francis and Stephen Shute on Bowden Hill. In August 1826 the property was sold, the business having been declared bankrupt. However, flax must also have been manufactured in or near the town as late as 1841, as in the census of that year a number of young girls gave their occupation as flax-factory workers, but there is no trace of where this factory was located. The production of flax needs a good supply of water, so it is probable that it was based at one of the mills in the Fordton area.

Considering the importance of the industry and the wealth produced by it over such a lengthy period, it is sad that there is little trace of it left in the town. Some of the linhays off the High Street remain as a reminder, but they bear little resemblance to what they were like 200 or more years ago. One such linhay is behind No. 42 High Street; called Albert Place in 2004, it was formerly known as Hooker's Linhay after the family of master weavers who lived in No. 42. There were three cottages in the linhay, with three rooms in each. The families lived on the upper floor and the ground floor contained the looms at which they spun the cloth. They worked from around 5.30 in the morning until 6.30 in the evening and at 7.00p.m. the iron gate and the heavy wooden door behind it leading into the High Street would be locked by the master, making the workers and their families virtual prisoners in their homes. The ground floors of all the buildings were connected, allowing the master to walk from the main house through the lower floor of the linhay cottages, so not only were the workers virtual prisoners, they were also deprived of any real privacy.

The ground at the top end of the linhay was used to lay out the 'straddles', where the fuller would stretch out the woven material he had washed and leave it to dry. The hooks on which the cloth was secured were called tenterhooks, which is where we get the expression 'to be on tenterhooks'. The ground stretching up towards Barnfield behind the High Street would have been ideal for this purpose. Peoples Park was also once used for this purpose, hence its former name of 'The Racks'.

*Fordson Major Farm Tractor, with German POW 'Heinz' driving.* (MICHAEL LEE)

The townspeople were not always prepared to put up with their lot peacefully. In 1720 it is said that some 2,000 Kirton weavers went on strike for higher wages which they secured by standing firm for a fortnight. Similar unrest occurred in 1726 – this time the ringleaders were imprisoned, but the mob refused to be quelled. They surrounded the courthouse and pelted the justices with stones. The 'constables' were so afraid of the mob that the prisoners were released.

Although life was hard for the workers in the industry there were fortunes to be made. The Tuckfields, of Little Fulford, were among the most prominent, as were the Davies of Creedy. The Northcote family, at one time of Newton St Cyres and now Earls of Iddesleigh, also prospered in the wool industry.

## The Leather Trade

The tanner or currier has been a fixture in the town since the late-sixteenth century and the last tannery, that of Bruce Adams, only closed in 1964. According to Major Venn the first recorded tanner in Crediton was William Squire who died in 1586. The job of the tanner was to convert cowhides into leather. It was a long and quite complex process which involved periods of immersion in limepits, washing and drying. A good supply of water was needed for the process as well as a supply of bark (traditionally from oak trees).

At one time there were four tanneries in the town, in Porch Court off the High Street, in Parliament Street, near East Street on the site of Hayward's School, and on Bowden Hill. We have fairly detailed knowledge of three of these.

The tannery off the High Street was a family business founded by Edward Adams in 1792. It closed as recently as 1964 when Bruce Adams retired. In the nineteenth century William Adams worked in close co-operation with Samuel Gimblett who had a shoe factory behind the Town Hall, and most of the leather he produced was turned into boots and shoes there. Indeed, a rail was laid down from the tan pit to the shoe factory in order to easily transport the cured hides. It is said that this rail has never been taken up.

The Parliament Street tannery buildings remained to an even later date, only being demolished in 1976. However, for the last 50 years of their life they were used as a council storehouse and yard. The building was first used as a tannery by Samuel Roberts in 1790. He lived in the Thatched House in Belle Parade. The site had several owners including John Francis, who in the 1830s opposed the construction of Union Road as his 'wash' on Bowden Hill would be cut off from the tannery and thus his property would be 'impoverished'. In later years the 'wash' was situated roughly where the bowling-green lies in 2004. In 1879 Mr William Snell bought the business. He lived at No. 129 High Street where he and his father had been running a small tanning business for some time. Operations were transferred to the much larger Parliament Street site and the house in the High Street was used as a shop and office. His diary records that on 29 March 1879 'we took in 6 hides and 3 veal skins this day from Tavistock market, and Mr John Snell went to Bristol and bought 62 hides... The first commencement of our tanning.' However, 1879 was apparently not a very good year for the tanner, or for farmers for that matter. In his diary entry for 30 June he complains that:

*... rain still continues to fall every day, and we have had nothing but wet weather for the last six months. Very bad bark harvest, and farmers' land is an awful mess. Cannot till turnips or work on land in any way...*

The earliest record we have of the East Street tan yard is from 1775 when the business was sold as a going concern on the death of Robert Stone to John Pring. The last owner was a Mr George Melhuish who took over the bankrupt business in 1811. Mr Melhuish must also have found it a struggle as 11 years later, in 1822, the tannery was finally wound up in bankruptcy. Melhuish also ran a brick-making business which appears to have been more successful.

## Boots and Shoes

The boot and shoe trade grew in Crediton to replace the failing woollen industry in the early part of the nineteenth century. It was at first mainly a cottage industry, but in the latter years of the century a few of the more enterprising shoemakers or cordwainers started to centralise their operations in factories. At the close of the nineteenth century there were five factories in the town and, together with many surviving 'cottage' operations, employed over 400 men and women, around 20 per cent of the working population.

In the early years of the industry the description 'cordwainer' was frequently used. The word is thought to be of Norman French origin, and the implication was that the cordwainer was a superior craftsmen, one who worked the leather, as opposed to the plain shoemaker.

Mechanisation came late to the industry, mainly due to the inconsistency of the quality of the leather produced in those days, and the varying shape and size of the human foot. For many years the factories and cottage operations worked closely together with work being passed out by the factory owners on a sort of piecework basis. In Bowden Hill and parts of Park Street shoemaking was the occupation of the family in nearly half of the houses.

Kenneth Hudson, in his book *Towards Precision Shoemaking*, tells of the conditions in those times. The uppers were cut in the factory and then sent to the outworkers in their homes:

*Under the outworking system, many of the masters drank heavily for two or three days after they had made their weekly deliveries to the factories and collected their money. Their apprentices, boys of twelve to fourteen, or even younger, were compelled to be idle during their master's drinking bouts and then had to work day and night in order to catch up with their new week's stint.*

As mechanisation grew the factory system started to take over; with both masters and apprentices under the supervision of the factory owner the pace of work could be controlled 'and exploitation of child labour was prevented.' The invention of the sewing machine brought increased mechanisation to the shoemaking operation and with it the introduction of women into the trade; almost all machinists were female.

As was said earlier there were five factories in the town in the 1890s. Two belonged to the Elston brothers whose father originated from the Bowden Hill area of the town. Their father John built the first factory in the town in Parliament Street at the bottom of Deep Lane opposite Snell's Tannery. The site had previously been the Union Inn which had burnt down and been rebuilt. It is said that the Elston's factory was the first to have machinery in the South West. John Elston was killed in an accident in Barnstaple in 1891. His great-granddaughter, Winnie Davey, is still alive and living in the Gloucester area at the time of writing.

*Girls at work in the machine room of Gimblett's Economic Shoe Works at 112 High Street.* (MARY BLAMEY)

The two sons built factories of their own, both of which are still standing in 2004. Harry Elston built what, in 2004, is Redvers House in Union Road, and for much of the twentieth century it was owned by Jackson's. Fred also built a factory in Union Road at the top of Church Street; in 2004 a tool-hire company, it was also for many years a steam laundry and later a garage.

Following the Boer War, in which it is said that the boots worn by both sides of the conflict had been made in Crediton, some members of the Elston family emigrated to South Africa. Members of the Harvey family who lived on Bowden Hill and were also well known in the town as shoemakers, but who remained operating as a cottage industry, emigrated along with them. They based their new operations in Port Elizabeth and set up successful factories and retail outlets. The names of Elston and Harvey are still remembered in that town for their shoe production.

Fred Elston emigrated to Canada but Harry continued production in Crediton until he retired and his factory closed in 1914. Harry held out for as long as he could in the face of strong competition from the larger operations, mainly in Northampton. If he could have held out for a few months longer, demand for boots for the soldiers during the First World War might have kept his workforce fully occupied for longer, and the business may just have survived.

Samuel Gimblett was another of the factory owners. He was not a local man, but originated from St Clements in Cornwall. The story goes that in 1868 he was planning to emigrate but missed his ship, and being a religious man he took this as a sign. Looking for a place to launch a business he was passing through Crediton when he spotted a building for sale. He alighted from his carriage and negotiated the purchase on the spot. Soon afterwards he built his 'Economic Shoe Works' near the High Street, behind No. 112. He was said to be a good employer and built a social club and coffee shop for his workers. The coffee shop was called the Buller's Arms, but as Gimblett was a strict Nonconformist it is unlikely that the premises sold anything alcoholic. Gimblett lived to the age of 86, and after he died in 1906 his son Richard took over, but it was said that he did not have his father's business acumen and he quickly sold the business to the Park Brothers, who only continued trading for a short while, before they too emigrated to South Africa taking some of the workforce with them.

Less is known about the other two large factories. One was at 34 High Street next to the White Swan. It was owned by William Dodderidge and was operational between 1871 and the 1890s. Also, the 1851 census records a John Park, shoemaker, at this address. The other large factory was in Bell Court

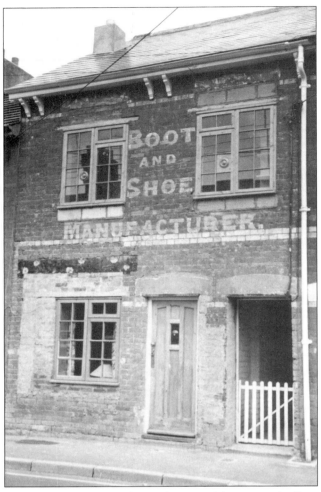

*Whilst repairs were taking place on this cottage in East Street in 1995 it was revealed that it had been used as a boot and shoe factory. The business was probably run by a Mr George Elston.* (BABS STUTCHBURY)

near the Congregational Church and was owned by James Sprague. There were several other smaller factories operating out of premises no larger than a single house, but nevertheless employing a number of hands – one such was in East Street.

## Millers and Milling

Wheat and four milling was another important local industry. The mills owned by W. & J. Drake, and later by John Carthew at Four Mills, produced flour for the bakers until they were destroyed by fire in the 1880s. Downes Mill was the home of the Mallett family for many generations, possibly as far back as 1545, and although in the later years it was no longer a working mill the family lived there until the 1970s. At the time of writing the property is owned by Ladds who run a gunsmiths and computer business from the premises. Fordton Mill is still operational, and over the years has served a number of purposes,

mainly as a flour mill, but also a sawmill and a producer of flax.

## Confectionery and Lozenges

### ERNEST JACKSON & CO.

For significant parts of the twentieth century Ernest Jackson & Co. was the largest employer in the town, yet the history of the company goes back much further. In 1817 William Searle, a local chemist, began making medicinal lozenges behind what is now 29 High Street. The main products in those days were barley sugars and blackcurrant-flavoured lozenges. It was not until 1891 that Ernest Jackson bought the company from Searle.

It grew and prospered and in 1917 took over the former boot factory in Union Road. In 1922 the company split into two groups – Ernest Jackson continued to supply the chemist trade and the Arcadian Works Ltd made lozenges. In 1923 the 'Throaties' brand was first launched with the claim that they 'went straight to the spot' of any cough or cold. This was Jackson's most successful product, and by the 1980s 'Throaties' were the leading brand of medicated pastille in the country.

In the early part of the twentieth century a factory girl at Jackson's would earn between 7s. (35p) and 10s. (50p) per week, working from 7a.m to 7p.m Monday to Friday, and 7a.m. to 4p.m. on Saturday. There was a 45-minute breakfast break and one hour for lunch, but no tea breaks. A whistle would be sounded at 7a.m. to signal the start of work and again at 8.30a.m. to indicate the start of the breakfast break.

It is said that in those days the workforce would absentee themselves from work at haymaking time, and that Mr Jackson was unconcerned by this.

In the postwar period the weekly hours were less, but older Kirtonians will remember the factory siren sounding regularly at 8a.m., 1p.m., 2p.m. and 5p.m. each weekday, signalling the start and end of morning and afternoon shifts; also the mass exodus from the gates at the end of each shift, with any unsuspecting visitor unaware of this daily ritual being liable to be run over in the rush of departing workers.

In 1973 the company sold the factory in Union Road and expanded the main High Street works. In 1980 William Jackson died and a few years later, in 1984, the company was sold to Bassett Foods plc. In 1989 Bassett's were taken over by Cadbury Schweppes. In 2004 the company does not employ anywhere near the same number of people that it did in its heyday, but it remains a significant employer in the town.

Medicinal
## LOZENGES
and
## PASTILLES

made by
### ERNEST JACKSON & Co., Ltd.
Manufacturing Chemists

CREDITON                    DEVON

Established 1817

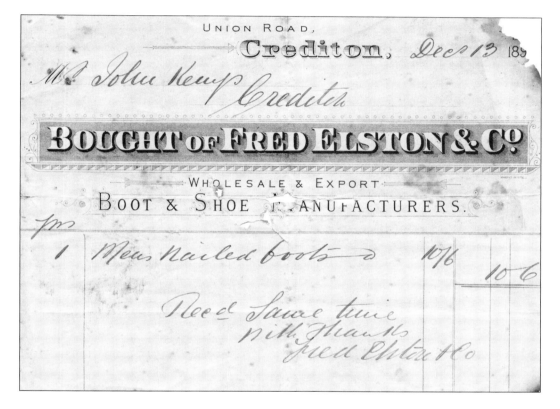

UNION ROAD,
Crediton, Dec 13 18__

M* John Kemp
Crediton

# BOUGHT of FRED ELSTON & Co.

WHOLESALE & EXPORT
BOOT & SHOE MANUFACTURERS.

1   Mens Nailed boots        10/6        10 6

Rec'd Same time
with thanks
Fred Elston & Co

*Everyone helps with haymaking in 1913. (CAHMS, PHOTO BERRY)*

## BRISTOW'S OF DEVON (FORMERLY JOHN CLEAVE (DEVON) LTD)

John Cleave (Devon) Ltd was founded in 1881 and traded from the old Palace Works, situated to the east of the Parish Church and on part of the site now occupied by the milk factory. The company prospered largely due to an agreement negotiated by Charles Saddler Bristow with Jacques Farvarages in 1902 to introduce Swiss milk chocolate into Britain. Cleave's were the first company to manufacture this product in the country. In 1927 the company was showing signs of failing and Charles Bristow returned to Crediton in a vain attempt to revive the business, but it fell victim to the depression and was finally liquidated in 1931. He bought a section of the Palace Works, and in February 1932 commenced the manufacture of Bristow's Devonshire Butterscotch. Shortly after this his youngest son, George Bristow, returned from South Africa and a career in shipping to become responsible for building up the business. He added other hard-boiled sweets, then Devon toffee, and finally clotted-cream fudge to the list of products manufactured.

The business outgrew the Palace Works and in 1950 a new factory was built in Mill Street. Later, due to yet further expansion, another site was found at Lord's Meadow in 1962. This was built in the middle of a farmer's field, to later be surrounded by other businesses in what was to become the Lord's Meadow Industrial Estate.

*A 'fleet' vehicle of the pre-war period.* (FRANK BRISTOW)

*The vehicle fleet outside the Mill Street factory.*
(FRANK BRISTOW)

*The packing room at Bristow's Palace Works, sometime between 1935 and 1950.* (FRANK BRISTOW)

In 1977 Bristow's developed a new process for the manufacture of wrapped fudge, and as a result they became recognised as the leading fudge manufacturer in the country. To this was also added export contracts and the manufacture of fudge for other large confectionery makers. During this period Bristow's acquired three other confectionery companies – Cameo of Edinburgh, giving it a Scottish base; Pollards of Newton Abbot, the other main sugar confectionery manufacturer in Devon; and Tuckers of Totnes, one of the oldest confectionery companies in the country, founded in 1800. With these acquisitions, including the transfer of all production to Crediton, came a new product, toffee bonbons. The sum of all these developments within the company, run at the time of writing by George Bristow's two sons, Kenneth and Frank, brought production to the astonishing level of one million sweets per day. In 2004 Bristow's can boast an international reputation for their toffee and fudge products.

## DEVON PACK FREEZE

The company was started in 1947 by Mr Henry Adams at 55 East Street. He had a greengrocery, poultry and rabbit business which supplied hotels and restaurants in the district. The idea of deep freezing was relatively new and he got together with Henry Lee of Dowrich, Bill Sutton (the manager of Ambrosia at Lapford) and others to form Devon Pack Freeze, with Arthur King Robinson as secretary.

They soon outgrew these premises and within a year purchased the old slaughterhouse in Station Yard. The slaughterhouse was extended and refrigeration units built. In the first year of operations at the station they processed 150 tons of frozen vegetables, with the hope of adding poultry and rabbit to the organisation in the future. In the early days there were problems with the equipment. In particular with the 'pea viner', which was unable to tell the difference between weeds and peas, and for some time the peas had to be processed by hand. At one time they got so far behind that the peas were around two weeks old before they were frozen.

Machinery and quality control improved over the years, and for a while the company was quite successful. However, Devon Pack Freeze never moved beyond vegetable production. After only a few years the company was taken over by Devon & Cornwall Poultry Ltd who continued to use the freezing plant, but for poultry. Later this group was bought out by Shipphams who operated the plant successfully for many years, and for at least part of their tenure were the largest employers in the town.

Shipphams ceased production in Crediton in the 1990s.

## Graphics plc

At the time of writing Graphics have taken over the mantle of the largest employer in the town, and the company is continuing Crediton's history of innovative manufacturing. Throughout the 1990s Graphics was one of the fastest-developing technology companies in the South West, employing well over 100 local people, producing printed circuits and computerised systems for many major companies and for the British Army. The owner, Mr Rex Rosario, was recently awarded the OBE for services to the electronics industry.

*Rex Rosario* OBE, *owner of Graphics plc, discusses a point with the Princess Royal on her visit to the factory in November 2002.* (CREDITON COUNTRY COURIER)

The company is prepared to contribute to the community by sponsoring football and rugby teams in the town, and the international bowler Ian Bond, who is an employee.

## Builders

Crediton has been well served by building companies for centuries, and a ready supply of stone and brick has been available for them to carry out their work. The quarry at Posbury has been worked since time immemorial and many local buildings, including the Parish Church, and the majority of the miles of stone wall that can be seen around the town were constructed from Posbury stone.

Following two disastrous fires in the eighteenth century the majority of new buildings in the High Street were constructed of brick. There are three known sites of brickworks in Crediton – at St Lawrence Green, on the site of the Market Street Car Park, and near Downes Head. In 2004 no trace of any of these works remain, but they must have been working at full capacity to meet the demand for rebuilding the town in the dark days following those fires.

### DART & FRANCIS

William Dart returned from London in 1854 and originally set up business behind 117 High Street. He later moved to 'Voler's Yard' behind 127 and 128 High Street where the company continued to trade until it closed in 1986.

In 1881 Sidney Francis came to Crediton and started work with the firm. In 1903 he married William Dart's daughter Alice and became a partner in the company, and thus Dart & Francis was born. For a short while between 1900 and 1903 Mr Dart took on a Mr Pike as a partner. The only major contract in that period was restoration work on the Redcliffe Hotel in Paignton, and a plaque still stands in that hotel stating that Dart & Pike of Crediton completed the work.

The company rapidly gained a reputation for the quality of its work, especially in the ecclesiastical field and the restoration of buildings. Dart & Francis stonemasons and woodcarvers were in demand all over England and later across the world.

One of the earliest major contracts was to build the Exminster Asylums in the 1860s. The company was also asked to restore the Theatre Royal in Exeter after the disastrous fire of 1887 which resulted in the death of 160 members of the audience. Dart & Francis built the present St David's Church in Exeter in the early years of the twentieth century and helped

*Heaton Satchville in North Devon, built by Dart &*
*Francis in the early years of the twentieth century for Lord*
*Clifford.* (ALAN DISCOMBE)

with restoration work on Exeter Cathedral after the war. In the early 1900s they built Heaton Satchville in North Devon for Lord Clinton and rebuilt Creedy House for Sir Patrick Ferguson Davie after the disastrous fire there in 1915.

At its height the company had three premises in Crediton. As well as the yard behind the High Street the partners owned an orchard stables and stone yard in Union Road (now the site of a cycle shop) and a yard at the railway station. At its peak the company was also a significant employer in the town and 49 members of their staff served in the First World War, seven of whom did not return.

In the 1950s a Mr Staddon took over the firm and in 1961 it passed to its last owner, Alan Discombe. During his time Dart & Francis carried out work on Guildford and Liverpool Cathedrals and the London Guildhall. The Guildhall contract was carried out under the guidance of the architect Sir Giles Scott and took 2½ years to complete.

Locally there are many fine examples of Dart & Francis' work to be seen – the Mount, part of the Grammar School boarding-houses; Mount Jocelyn, built for the Jacksons; and four properties in Peoples Park Road – The Orchard, The Gables, Pharelands and Ravensworth. The firm also built Holy Trinity Church at Yeoford.

Although the company has ceased to trade, these and other fine buildings stand as memorials to the craftsmanship of Dart & Francis' workforce; and not just in this country. The war memorial in Valetta Cathedral, Malta and the barrelled ceiling in St George's Cathedral in Jerusalem are examples of their work that can be seen abroad.

## BERRY & VINCENT

Berry & Vincent are the oldest building firm in the town that is still trading at the time of writing. The firm is

believed to have been started by a John Prawl in around 1770. He lived in Park Street near the junction with Bowden Hill. Prawl was succeeded by John Berry, a former apprentice who married his daughter in 1803.

John was succeeded by his son, William, and under his direction the firm was heavily involved in the building of the Exeter and North Devon Railway line. Berry & Vincent constructed some 20 bridges on the line and Crediton Station buildings, said to be to a design by Brunel. They also built Newton St Cyres Station and one at Cowley Bridge. William also moved the workshops from a site near the Green to its present location on the corner of Union Road and Church Street when the land was purchased to make way for the new Grammar School in 1860.

William's eldest son, William Boddy Berry, took over from his father and during his time in charge of the firm, work completed included the refurbishment of the Lady Chapel after the Grammar School had moved out.

The next generation of the family to take on the business came in the form of Hubert Berry in 1907. In 1908 he designed and built the concrete bridge over the River Exe at Thorverton. This is the oldest reinforced-concrete bridge in Devon, possibly in the country, and only recently has it needed strengthening to cope with the ever-increasing weight of the lorries on our roads. In 1909 he designed and built the Churchworker's Institute on the crest of the hill in Union Road.

Edwin Reginald Vincent became a partner in 1923 and the firm changed its name to Berry & Vincent in 1934. For a short period in the 1960s they merged with White & Sons, another local building firm, and took on the name White & Vincent. This merger did not last for many years and both companies went their separate ways reverting back to their former names.

In recent times their most notable work has been the Catholic Church of St Boniface in Park Street.

## A. WHITE & SONS

White's are the youngest of the established builders in Crediton. The founder, Albert White, was a very enterprising carpenter who was prepared to speculate, and on most occasions he did so with success. He was the son of a shoemaker, Thomas White, who lived in Kiddicott. He started the company in 1921 and later in that decade bought 'Belmont' in Searle Street. He converted the house into two dwellings and built the company workshop and offices on ground to the rear of the building which stretched up to Peoples Park Road. The firm are still using the

**Above:** *Preparation work in Dart & Francis' yard, c.1950s. Charlie Butt is on the left, behind the massive tree stump is Harold Davey and holding the axe is Bill Lovegrove.* (RON HAMLIN)

**Left:** *A view of St George's Cathedral in Jerusalem. The barrelled ceiling was provided by Dart & Francis.*
(ALAN DISCOMBE)

**Below:** *Berry & Vincent yard on the corner of Church Street and Union Road. Motor vehicles and telephone wires apart, this is a view that has changed little in over 100 years.*

same offices in 2004. White's were undertakers as well as builders from the very beginning, Albert's training as a carpenter made sure of that. Albert also bought the Newcombes estate but did not keep the house and gardens for very long. He did, however, retain the ground behind the house, and there he built the houses in Albert Road. He also built Kenwyn Nursing Home in 1937 where many Kirtonians of a certain age will have been born.

Albert's eldest son, Tom, joined the firm at the age of 14 and like his father was apprenticed as a carpenter. He died in 2003 at the age of 91. His younger son, also called Albert but known to all as Bert, did not join the company immediately, instead training as an architect. In 1946 he did join up with his elder brother and it was from this period that the business really started to expand. In the years following the war there was a great demand for housing and White's constructed a good deal of the council properties built in the late 1940s and '50s. They built all of Winswood and much of the Butt Parks estate.

As mentioned previously, the 1960s brought a short, but not altogether successful, amalgamation with another local builder, Berry & Vincent, under the name of White & Vincent. Both companies soon went their separate ways again and reverted to their former titles.

In 1970 David White, eldest son of Bert, joined the firm, thus bringing the third generation of the family into the business, and in 1979 his younger brother, Andrew, also came on board. Andrew is also a church governor, following his father into that role.

The nature of the company has changed over the years with a move first towards private estate work and later to mainly contracting. However, White's still have a loyal and long-serving workforce. Terry Stoneman retired from the firm after 50 years and Bill Clarke, who still works for them in 2004, is fast approaching that milestone.

There have been many other building firms in the town worthy of note. Hopkin's traded for many years of the twentieth century. The Rodd brothers also ran a successful business from their premises in Market Street. In 2004 the tendency is towards contract work, and family businesses of the nature of Berry & Vincent, Dart & Francis, Hopkin's, Rodd's and A. White & Sons are becoming something of a rarity. Building workers today tend to be hired for the length of a contract and then move on to the next job.

## Kirton Kayaks

When Tony Snell started building canoes in 1965, along with his father Bill, in a shed behind Mill Street Garage, he could hardly have thought that the company would grow to have an international reputation in the world of canoeing. Unfortunately, although Tony saw the company blossom and grow, he did not live long enough to see the fulfilment of what he had started in such humble surroundings.

By 1969 he had outgrown the shed and had erected a workshop behind the egg-packing station on the new Lord's Meadow Trading Estate. Within just a few years the packing station was taken over for further expansion.

In 1970 Dave Green (an international canoeist who paddled Tony's canoes and was an owner of the

*The council-houses at Winswood under construction shortly after the end of the war. The photo was taken from Butt Parks. (DAVID WHITE)*

Twickenham Canoe Centre), joined the firm and moved with his family to Crediton. With Dave's knowledge and influence in the canoeing world and Tony's skill (he had been an apprentice carpenter with Dart & Francis before he turned his hand to fibreglass) the company soon acquired the world-wide licence to build Struer and Klepper designs. In those days Struer was the top name in the world of canoe racing, and in 2004 the Klepper contract is still bringing in money through sales to the military.

Tony died in 1973 but, despite this loss, the company prospered until the mid-1980s when polythene started to replace fibreglass as the main ingredient to make canoes. Until that time the company was employing 15 staff who were producing 20 canoes per week. For a period of around 10 years there was hardly a canoe race held anywhere in the world without a Crediton-built boat finishing in the top three, and often taking all three podium places.

In 1989 the fall of the Berlin Wall hit Kirton Kayaks hard. Canoeing is a major sport in many Eastern European countries and now canoes made in Poland are being used by all the top international canoeists.

The company, although much smaller at the time of writing, is still keeping Crediton on the map and is run by Peter Cockram, a local man, who joined the firm as a 16-year-old straight, from school. Dave Green has retired, but still sits on the British Canoe Union marathon-racing committee and is an international judge.

*Dave Green, in the rear seat, with his international racing partner Martin Bosher, c.1970.* (DAVE GREEN)

*Bill Snell at work in the Lord's Meadow Factory, c.1970.* (DAVE GREEN)

*Tony Snell, founder of Kirton Kayaks, c.1970.*

(DAVE GREEN)

## Chapter 8

◇

# Fire, Flood and Plague
## and the People of the Rescue Services

## Ordeal by Fire

In times past Crediton has had a reputation for the frequency and severity of its fires. The earliest recorded fire was in 1710, which broke out in Porch Court in the West Town. Later in the same year, on 19 December, another fire destroyed a house, stabling and much other property 'about the middle of the market'. A family of three – John Cobley, his son also called John and Mary his daughter – all perished in the first fire. Revd Thomas Ley, preaching at the funeral of this unfortunate family, described the fire as threatening destruction to a great part of the town, as it was fanned by very strong winds. However, there was heavy rain falling when the fire broke out and it was this that confined it to one house.

The town was not so fortunate with the 1743 fire as it followed a period of drought and therefore spread rapidly through the dry thatched and timbered properties. The fire was of sufficient severity to have been reported in the national press with the *Universal Spectator* of 3 September reporting that:

*... there is not a house standing in all the town, from the sign of The Lamb [in North Street] to the utmost end of The Green (which is half a mile), together with all back-lets, lanes, lineys, gardens and apple-trees; the apples roasting as they hung.*

A few days after this terrible conflagration Revd Miciah Towgood, a well-known Dissenting minister, preached a sermon, in part condemning the people of the town and calling on them to mend their sinful ways. He began by describing Crediton as 'a flourishing town sunk in a few hours into a ruinous heap.' He went on to say that it was not chance that brought this to the town but a judgement. It is thought that the fire started in a house where some 'heathenish fellows' were playing cards on a Sunday, and it was fat from a joint of meat being roasted as a prize for the winner of the game that caused the initial spark.

Towgood went on in his sermon to criticise the people of Crediton for the drunkenness, general disorder and excesses in the town at the St Lawrence Fair the week before the fire, and he saw it as no coincidence that it started on the day that it did.

His sermon was also an appeal for charity. The people of Exeter were among the first to respond, raising around £500 in just a few days. Several other local towns also responded, as did Bristol and London, among more distant places.

The town had barely recovered from this tragedy when another fire broke out on 1 May 1769. This destroyed many recently rebuilt houses in an area stretching from North Street to around where No. 31 High Street stands in 2004. A conveyancing document of the same year gives some idea of what the people of the town must have faced during these years. This document does not give a precise location of the property other than it was situated near 'the Clockhouse in the West Town and Borough of Crediton.' The document refers to land:

*... whereon several Dwellinghouses and Gardens... formerly stood... all which premises were burnt down and destroyed in the fire at Crediton which happened [14 August 1743] and which were afterwards rebuilt and then burnt down and destroyed again in the fire at Crediton which happened on the first day of May last.*

A contemporary report states that the 1769 fire started at the house of one R. Pulman, a baker, and was caused by him drawing the fuel out of the oven before it had cooled, a spark flying up and catching the thatch alight. In this fire no fewer than 131 houses were destroyed, but only one life was lost; that of a very old man who was confined to his bed. Another account suggests that properties stretching from the top of Bowden Hill to the corn market and all of Back Lane (North Street), were destroyed. The person who wrote this account stated that their house and its contents were all destroyed and 'we have lain in a orchard for two days and one night.' Once again

*Crediton Fire Brigade proudly show off their new engine. The date on the front of the appliance is 1877.  Left to right: E. Parry Jones, Mr Hedger, Mr Tothill (Bugler), ?, ? Mr Boddy, Firemaster Dr Heyman, ?.  (CREDITON FIRE BRIGADE)*

Exeter came to the rescue, sending a detachment of 100 soldiers to help.

These two fires account for the lack of ancient buildings in the High Street.  Virtually all properties post-date these fires – indeed a brick embedded into the wall at the rear of No. 129 High Street (formerly Summerwell's) bears the date 1776.

These fires were the most severe, but there are also reports of fires in the town in 1725 and 1772. The latter of these started at the King's Arms and spread to some 40 houses.  In the first half of the nineteenth century there are also reports of numerous fires.  An anonymous writer in 1852 stated that during the previous 20 years 'about one-half of the houses in the East Town, and a considerable part of those in The Green have been built on the charred ruins of former ones.'

The problem of fires was addressed in the Crediton Improvement Act which ordered that no new houses within the town were to be built with a thatched roof.  That Act also provided for a fire-engine for the town.

There is some doubt as to the location of the first fire station in the town.  However, all but one known record places it behind the Town Hall where the Conservative Club stands at the time of writing.  There is no doubt whatsoever that the engine was lodged there for many years, but an 1888 Ordnance Survey map of the town clearly shows the fire-engine house located at or near 65 High Street.  The next location for the engine was at the site of Snell's old tannery at the foot of Deep Lane, near where the library stands in 2004.  When the tannery closed in about 1924 the land was bought by Crediton Urban District Council and

used as a council yard, and a garage facing almost directly up Deep Lane was used to house the fire-engine.  The first motorised engine, a Dennis, was garaged there.

In 1924, however, the engine was still horse-drawn and the horses were housed at the stables of the Ship Hotel.  Les Berry remembers a gentleman called 'Buckie' Forward who used to ride around the town on a bicycle blowing his bugle to summon the fire-fighters.  Also someone used to run to the Ship to advise how many horses were required to pull the engine.  Walter Radford was the man in charge of the horses at the Ship, and it was often his team of animals that pulled the appliance, with him at the reins.  Walter was the town's last surviving horse 'cabby' who used to regularly meet trains at the station and convey passengers up to the town.  He died in 1936.

For a short period, including during the Second World War, the engine was housed in Exhibition Road.  After the war the station was moved to North Street.  Ivor Coram remembers it there when he moved into his shop next door in 1950.  In 2004 the site is a furniture shop.  A new fire station was built on the site of the old market in the 1960s and is still sited there at the time of writing.  However, a new station is under construction in Charlotte Street.

Crediton's fire-fighters have always been a voluntary brigade, the modern title being 'Retained Firemen'.  For much of the period between the wars the brigade captain was Mr E.F. Parry-Jones who lived in the Chantry in Dean Street.  He was succeeded by Mr G. Burrows.  During the latter part of the twentieth century Peter Howison was in charge under the new title of Station Commander. He retired in 2002 and was succeeded by Bob Kestell. In 2003 the brigade made news with the recruitment of Crediton's first female fire-fighter, Kate Bailey.

Although there have been some serious fires since the establishment of the town brigade there has been nothing on the scale of previous centuries. In 1886 four cottages in St Saviours 'Alley' were completely destroyed. The fire-engine was in attendance but was unable to deal with the blaze for over an hour because of a lack of water in the tank. A similar problem occurred when there was a fire at the White Hart in around 1930. The White Hart and a three-storey building opposite were almost totally destroyed. Ernest Vigers remembered that in those days, during dry spells in the summer, the water was cut off at times in order to conserve supplies. The hoses were run out but when they were turned on no water came forth. It was some time before someone could be found to turn the supply back on. Arthur King Robinson recalls that during this fire a leading fireman (possibly called Mr Kenshole) fell from a long ladder into the building behind a chimney. Miraculously he was not hurt and continued to fight the fire. Another story relating to this fire, told by Ernest Vigers, is of a sailor who frightened the watching crowd by climbing upon the remains of the wall and swaying as if he were about to fall off into the fire.

Involvement in the town brigade has been something of a family tradition. In 1887 the brigade was served by three members of the Wellacott family. In the postwar period Roger Steer followed his father 'Gifty' as station officer, and Alan Tonkin followed his father Albert, another station officer, into the brigade. Peter Howison also followed in his father's footsteps, as did Graham Frost. In 2004 the Smith brothers, Mark and Phil, are both members.

## A SHORT NARRATIVE OF THE TERRIBLE FIRE AT CREDITON

The following is a contemporary account by Miciah Towgood of the dreadful fire that swept through the West Town of Crediton on 14 August 1743. It is also an appeal for relief. The document is reproduced in its entirety with only a few grammatical and spelling changes to make it more easily understandable to a modern reader, but hopefully without losing the flavour of the time.

*Crediton, commonly called Kirton is one of the most ancient and populous towns in the west. In the times of the Saxon Kings, it was the flourishing see of the bishop, until King Edward the Confessor translated it to Exeter,* about the year 1050. *It was of old also famous for giving birth to St Winifred* (sic) [Boniface], *called the Apostle of Germany; because he converted the Hessians, Thuringians, and Frisians, to Christianity, and was canonised as a saint.*

*The town is divided into two parts, the eastern and the western: the latter of which is, by far, the most considerable for trade, for number of inhabitants, and for the beauty of its buildings as well as their extent. In this western part a very large and frequented market is kept, inferior, it is said to few in the Kingdom, as to two useful commodities, yarn and flesh. The populousness and importance of the place may be gathered from observing that fourteen or fifteen hundred serges are, one week with another, manufactured here, and sent abroad; and that some seventy bullocks, throughout the winter-quarter, is the weekly supply of their shambles.*

*This western town, as it is called, was one large and extended street, stretching from east to west, above half a mile in length, furnished with spacious and convenient market houses, and had a great number of courts and alleys branching from it, filled with many families of industrious poor.*

*About the middle part of this street, on the southern side, the fire broke forth, on Sunday August 14th, about eleven in the forenoon. The town has no supply of water but from pumps. A drought of several weeks had both much lessened that supply, and prepared the houses to receive and propagate the flame. The wind setting strong, at first from the north-east, and increasing with the fire, the desolation was carried from house to house, with amazing rapidity; so that the southern side, before it, was quickly all in flames. A little past noon, the wind veered towards the south, by which the fire was soon communicated to the north side of the street, so that all westward from the place of its first breaking out fell, in a few hours, prey to the raging element, and was turned into ashes.*

*Eastward, against the wind, it advanced with a slower pace; but neither engines, nor blowing up, nor any other means could stop its dreadful progress. It continued raging uncontrolled, till about eight in the evening, when it pleased God, at length, to stop its furious course.*

*The whole western town with its market houses and public buildings, a small part only excepted, now lies in the deepest ruins. The flames ran with such violence, flying over five or six houses at once, and kindling those beyond, that great quantities of goods, houses, apparel, looms with serges in them etc. were quickly destroyed. Besides many who were in the utmost danger, and were plucked as brands out of the burning, sixteen were already found to have perished in the desolation. Several others are missing, and supposed to be involved in the same fate.*

*Fire-damaged houses in the High Street in 1973. These houses were demolished to make way for the construction of St Saviours Way and Car Park.*
(MARGARET WOLLACOTT)

*Dealing with a fire in Park Street, 25 March 1922.*
(CAHMS, PHOTO BERRY)

*Crediton Fire Brigade in 2001.* Left to right, back row: *Allan 'Dick' Dendle, Phil Smith, Gary Grant, Kevin Grant, Richard Steer, Terry Phillips, Paul Newbery, Ian Salter, Sean Cooke, Alan Sweetland;* front row: *Mark 'Chubb' Ludgate, Chris Mitchell, Bob Kestell, Ally McDonald (Group Commander), Peter Howison, Richard Harling, Jeremy 'Biffo' Holland, Mark Smith, Roland 'Reg' Barker.* (CREDITON FIRE BRIGADE)

NEAR THIS SITE ON
SUNDAY AUGUST 14th. 1743
THE GREAT FIRE OF CREDITON STARTED
16 KYRTONIANS PERISHED
2000 WERE MADE HOMELESS
460 DWELLINGS WERE DESTROYED.

*Above: Dealing with a fire in a thatched cottage, July 1981.* (FIRE BRIGADE)

*Left: The plaque on the wall of 31 High Street marks the site where the 'great fire' of 1743 broke out.*

*In the widest part of the great street, which is nineteen yards in breadth, five persons were unawares hemmed in by the flames. They ran eastward and westward, but found themselves beat back by the fire raging beyond them, and no way to escape. In this horrible distress they continued for some time, deploring to each other their miserable fate. At length finding their case desperate, and unable any longer to bear the scorching heat, one of them broke through the burning ruins of an house whose flames were nigh spent and happily escaped. Another seeing him not return, and hoping he might possibly have found a passage through attempted the same and was also preserved. The remaining three fell a sacrifice and perished in the street.*

*At the western end of the town is a large and open field called The Green; above an hundred yards in length, and in breadth above forty-three, surrounded thick with houses. Thither the inhabitants brought and lodged their goods, not doubting but there they would be safe from the spreading flame; but even there also they were quickly seized; neither persons nor goods could stand before the sweeping deluge. The men were glad to escape with their lives as a prey, and the goods almost entirely consumed.*

*By this terrible calamity above four hundred and fifty families are turned out of their dwellings, a considerable part of which had, for some time, no lodging but the open field, nor any roof but the heavens. The inhabitants, to avoid all appearance of the common practice in such cases of over rating their loss, have in the opinion of numbers of competent and able judges, set it very much below the truth, at forty thousand pounds. The devastation has been measured, and for more than half a*

*mile on one side of the street not a single house is standing, nor scarce a bit of timber to be seen; and but a very small spot is left on the other. Those who have seen the late like desolation at Tiverton and Blandford, think this to be in compass equal to them both. A greater extent of ruins no fire, perhaps, since that of London, hath ever left behind it. Above two thousand of the poorer sort, who were before subsisted comfortably on their labour are now thrown at once on the compassions of the public, without which, many of them must quickly and inevitably perish for want.*

*A neighbouring city [Exeter], ever generous to the distressed, notwithstanding its great expense in building and supporting an hospital for the sick, exerted itself with a surprising and most seasonable vigour on this deplorable occasion, collecting, in a few days, more than five hundred pounds for the sufferers relief. Their case is now lying before London and Bristol, and will speedily be communicated to other principal towns, and their charity be entreated by recommendatory letters, not in the common method of briefs. With great thankfulness we acknowledge the spirit of uncommon compassion and liberality which has appeared in many places around us, as well as some noble benefactions sent by persons of high rank. It is hoped so uncommon a distress will move bowels of pity, and draw charitable supplies from distant parts of the land. And may God, in mercy, keep all other towns from the like calamitous stroke.*

*Note. Whatever charities are remitted to the Rev. Mr Stacey, or to Miciah Towgood, in Crediton, will be put into a common stock, and impartially distributed among the sufferers.*

*Crediton's first fire-engine in a photograph taken at Threshers, in a field called Dicky Docky, c.1860. (CAHMS)*

*Crediton Fire Brigade in 1877.* The picture includes: *C. Nankivell, S. Gillard, S. Wellacott, G. Beer, H. Butson, W. Loosemore, W. Harris, J. Wellacott, G. Jessop, H. Sanders, W. Wellacott, S. Horne, J. Harvey (Bugler), Captain William Heygate, Superintendant J. Templeton, Foreman T.H. White, Engineer Lewis Hicks* (CREDITON FIRE BRIGADE)

# Flood

Flooding in the town must have been a fairly regular occurrence in times gone by but, unlike those for fires, no records remain. The cottages at Fordton, built in around 1850, must have suffered on a regular basis, but the first occurrence known to the author is in the 1920s.

The East Town has also suffered on a number of occasions. In early July 1950 a local newspaper reported that a cloudburst from a 'funnel cloud' lasting no more than 20 seconds (surely a misprint), caused widespread flooding. A district nurse's car was swept down Bowden Hill, and houses in Mill Street were inundated with water and thick mud. It was reported that workers at the potato-crisp factory, also in Mill Street, had to run to safety 'before the rising flood water'. The Mill Street area was subject to regular flooding until the re-seweraging scheme was completed in the 1980s.

The worst floods of recent times occurred at Fordton in 1960 when, on 1 October, 2¼ inches of rain fell in 24 hours. Help came from RNAS Yeovilton who sent a team of five aircraftsmen with driers to dry out the cob buildings. Unfortunately the group of cob cottages which stood on the west side of the road were so badly damaged they had to be demolished. On 7 October the Urban District Council wrote thanking Yeovilton for the work the men had done in drying out almost 40 houses, and requested that the men be allowed to remain in the town as flooding had returned to the Fordton area. The railway line between Exeter and Crediton had to be closed because of structural damage to a bridge just upstream from Codshead Bridge.

In 1978 a flood-prevention scheme was completed – an overflow channel was built at Fordton Bridge, the weir which once supplied a head of water for the leat at Downes Mill was breached and the old Cosdshead Bridge was removed. This seems to have been successful as in October 2000, when the worst rains since 1960 occurred, apart from a small amount of water in the road the area was spared any serious flooding. That said, the town was virtually cut off as flooding near Downes Mill and at Creedy Bridge meant access to Exeter and Tiverton was impossible for many hours.

*Flooding at Fordton, probably in 1926.  (*Babs Stutchbury*)*

*Damage to the railway line at Codshead Bridge in the floods of October 1960.  (*Western Morning News*)*

*Tea for a stranded householder, Fordton, October 1960.  (*CAHMS*)*

## Plague

There are no surviving records of the affects of the Black Death of 1349 on Crediton, but it is virtually certain that the town was affected.

The sixteenth and seventeenth centuries saw many instances of plague sweeping through the country and records exist to show that Crediton did not escape – indeed populous urban areas were more susceptible than rural communities. The first serious strike on Crediton was in 1571 when over 540 deaths were recorded on the register, as compared to a normal amount of around 50. This visitation peaked in July, when some 140 burials were recorded, and continued into the following year. Although accurate population figures are not available for this time, it can be estimated that a figure of 540 deaths represents approaching 20 per cent of the population.

In 1591, just 20 years later, the attack was not quite so severe, but nevertheless over 400 burials were recorded. There were a further two lesser visitations in 1587/8 and 1596/7. Crediton was spared for the next 50 years, but plague reappeared in 1646 when over 250 people died in the town.

The 1665 plague, which affected almost the whole country, came to Crediton, but the records of that time are not as comprehensive as for the previous century, so the severity of its affect cannot be judged accurately.

Paul Slack has written a detailed account of the affect of these plagues, including figures for Crediton. He concluded that the 'plagues of 1571 and 1591/2 were two of the worst in any Devonshire parish... Crediton suffered four serious mortalities in a generation and there may have been others.'

Crediton seems to have largely escaped later outbreaks, for Towgood, in his sermon following the 1743 fire, gives thanks that we were largely unaffected by the recent 'malignant and sweeping sickness'. Also, our water-supply seems to have been sufficiently clean to avoid the cholera epidemics that affected much of the country, including Exeter where over 400 people died in the 1830s.

## Earthquake

In the early hours of the morning of 21 July 1827 Crediton was hit by an earthquake. Brice's journal reported that:

*... the houses and beds did tremble to such a degree as was ever known in the town. The pewter on the shelves was pistled together, as if a Pewterer had been sorting his goods. The Weaver's Looms (especially those in Chambers and Lofts) did shake in such a manner as to frighten the people. Boxes and Chests of Drawers were moved very strangely. It was felt many miles around us...*

*A protest about religious education outside Hayward's School. The banner reads 'Thy children be taught of The Lord'. The fountain is visible in the background so the photograph must have been taken after 1887. (CAHMS)*

# Chapter 9

## Education in Crediton

There are no records of a school in Crediton prior to 1547 when the Grammar School was founded under a charter of Edward VI. However, there certainly would have been some form of religious learning carried out ever since the foundation of the monastery in 739. There was a later decree of Queen Elizabeth I which confirmed the school's status and provided £8 per annum for the education of four poor boys of the town. It was from this charter that the school obtained its name. The Lady Chapel of the Parish Church was the schoolroom from 1572 until a new school was built near the Green in 1860.

The charter was the same as that which founded the Church Corporation, which meant that the church governors were in charge of the school. This situation remained until 1880 when a separate college of governors was set up to run the school, although many of them were also church governors. The school remained under the control of local people until 1923 when, under the Education Act of that year, it was handed over to the Local Education Authority.

Prior to 1860 Queen Elizabeth's School (QES) provided education for only a small number of children from the parish. There were charity schools, but they also only catered for small numbers. The first that we know of was the English School which was founded in 1630 from a sum of £20 donated by George Trowbridge. This school was sited near the foot of Bowden Hill. According to Charles Luxton this was truly a charity school for the poor of the town and 'it attracted many endowments'. It is said that in 1724 the school had 40 pupils, all boys, and the Grammar School had a similar number, so despite these many endowments the vast majority of the children of the town would have received no education at all. To qualify boys had to be of 'the Church of England' and were elected to attend; any absenteeism and the child was removed from the school to make way for a more 'deserving' pupil.

The next school to be founded was the Blue Coat School, which came into being in 1728 and stood on a site near the churchyard. In 1814 it was merged with the English School to become the Crediton United Charity School and moved to Penton House. At this time the infants' school was in Church Street in an area that forms the back of the graveyard in 2004. The house was demolished in the 1870s in order that the burial area might be extended.

Another charity school was founded in 1794 by Samuel Dunn, a teacher of mathematics and a Master of Longitude at Sea, who had moved to London in 1751. In his last will and testament he tells of his earlier life in Crediton. He recorded that at the time of the fire in 1743 he 'had been some time keeping a school' but then moved to 'the School House at the foot of Bowden Hill,' almost certainly the English School. He taught there until Christmas 1751.

Dunn owned property in Liverpool Street, London, and he willed a sum of £1,000 arising from this property; the capital from which would provide a salary of £30 per annum for a master to teach writing, lunar navigation, surveying and mathematics. He also provided for relatives in the town, one of whom was a John Harris to whom he bequeathed £20, plus a similar sum to be dispersed among his children. John Harris must have had a large family, for Dunn estimated that the children would get around £2 each. The Dunns School survived until 1911 at its site in Union Street. The last master was Mr Edmund Tompkins who then became a master at the Grammar School.

Hayward's School was opened on 9 January 1860 and the United Charity School at Penton then closed. The house was converted into a private dwelling, which at the beginning of the twentieth century was occupied by Col L. Montague, a noted Crediton historian.

The story of how Hayward's came to be built is one that starts over 200 years earlier. In 1635 Sir John Hayward of Rochester in Kent sold property to Sir Richard Buller and others 'that they might apply it for charitable purposes in such parishes as they should see fit', but the parish of St Nicholas,

Rochester, had to be one of them. In 1822 it was decided after a lengthy court case that the proceeds should be divided equally between Rochester and Crediton. It was James Buller, the grandfather of Sir Redvers, who was instrumental in pursuing the case through the courts. The money was initially used to fund the school at Penton, but later the Court of Chancery ordered that the Penton School be sold and the funds of the charity used to found a public elementary school. Thus a new school was built opposite the Parish Church on the site of a former tannery.

Crediton, therefore, had a public elementary school in the town some 20 years before the Education Act of 1880 and this was largely due to the efforts of James Buller. His son James Wentworth Buller and Elias Tremlett were also heavily involved with the Court of Chancery, dealing with objections from Rochester. Rochester's loss was Crediton's gain.

Hayward's served the children of Crediton for just over 100 years. Its first headmaster was James Bradford who came from the Charity School at Penton. In 1862 he was succeeded by R.E. Hall, and in 1899 by E. Titcombe, but the headmaster that will be remembered by just about every Kirtonian aged over 50 in 2004 was Charles Luxton. In addition to his work as headmaster, he was also a noted scholar of early history and his researches into the origins of Crediton are still valued in 2004, half a century after they were written. He was also a member of the town cricket team.

It was Mr Hall who enrolled the nine-year-old Ernest Bevin into the school in 1890. The young Bevin went on to have an illustrious career in politics, serving in Churchill's War Cabinet as Minister of Labour, and after the war in Atlee's Labour Government as Foreign Minister. In the 1930s he was secretary of the Transport and General Workers Union. Undoubtedly he was Hayward's most notable pupil.

However, by the time Hayward's reached its century it no longer met the needs of a growing population and an increasingly demanding education system. By the 1950s Crediton was in desperate need of a new school. At the enquiry held in the mid-1950s Dr Daniel Cook, the Deputy Chief Education Officer, said that Hayward's was overcrowded 'and the Boys School housed in very poor buildings.' He went on to say that:

*... a large number of children in Crediton and district are at present denied facilities for secondary education of a kind now provided throughout almost the whole of this County.*

A sad epitaph on a school building that once had been ahead of its time.

At the time of writing the former Hayward's Boys School buildings house a youth centre, drama centre and a pre-school playgroup amongst other activities, so they are still providing a useful service to the young of the town. The Hayward's name, of course,

**Crediton Church Boys Sunday School assembled in Hayward's School playground, 21 May 1909.**
(MARGARET WOLLACOTT)

still remains with the junior school that is housed in buildings mainly constructed in 1937. However, overcrowding was not solved completely when the new school was provided, because 'temporary' huts constructed in 1948 remained in use until 2003 when they were finally replaced by new classrooms.

In the 1950s three sites were considered for a new school: at the top of Barnfield near Back's Barn; Forches Cross and Exhibition Road. The school governors favoured the Barnfield site, but the County Council thought the one at Exhibition Road best. For once the 'locals' won the day and Shelley School, named after one of the governors Sir John Shelley, was opened on 19 October 1962 by Sir John himself. The new school was originally built to house up to 450 pupils.

For the whole of its existence the Grammar School was for the education of boys only. Prior to the latter years of the nineteenth century there was no public provision for the education of girls. During that century, however, there were private establishments in the town to which the daughters of the middle classes could be sent. Elizabeth Amery and later her daughter Ann kept a school for young ladies at No. 136 High Street, which was later run by the Row sisters. They ran the school for 41 years, finishing in 1910, 12 months before the High School opened. The sisters then sold No. 136 and retired to 11 Searle Street. On the other side of the High Street the Langworthy sisters kept a similar establishment at No. 13. In the middle of the nineteenth century this must have been a very successful establishment as, at one stage, they had over 20 boarders, more than the Grammar School had when it first moved to Western Road.

In 1911 the High School opened, at last providing secondary education for girls in the town. The school premises were partly funded by the County Council and partly by the Hayward's Charity. The school also had a mixed infants' section operating as a preparatory school for both the Grammar and High Schools.

Crediton had a number of preparatory schools in the twentieth century, including Crediton Preparatory School at the top of Searle Street. Also, Miss Louise Cornish started such a school on Bowden Hill in a building that later became the Crediton 'Over-60's Club'. In the 1920s she moved to the site of the former Gimblett's Economic Shoe Works; the entrance to the school being in Searle Street behind the Conservative Club. The school was sold to Miss Wright during the Second World War.

In 1965 the Grammar School and High School joined forces in a co-educational establishment – prior to that the sexes had been kept apart by a barbed-wire fence during school hours. Later government legislation brought an end to selective education in the town and from then the Grammar School and High Schools offered places to all the children of Crediton. Shelley became the school for the intermediate age group and the QES buildings for the senior and sixth-form pupils. In the 1980s the schools formed into a Community College with the purpose of also offering courses in skills and interests as well as academic subjects to adults.

The two remaining State-run primary schools are Hayward's and Landscore Schools. Landscore Infants School was built in 1880 to accommodate 120 children from the West Town. It has long since outgrown the small Victorian building in Landscore and has moved to a modern one in Threshers.

*Pupils in the playground at Hayward's School, c.1906.  (CAHMS)*

*Shelley School netball team, 1962–63.  Left to right, back row: Marion Wilcox, Rosalind Westcott, Margaret Hitchcock, Linda Strong; front row: Sheila Henderson, Mrs Norrish, Carol Keenor, Pam Manning, Liz Matthews.  (MR AND MRS A. HILL)*

*Shelley School under-16s football team, cup winners, 1962/3.  Left to right, back row: Brian Lemmy, Chris Theedom, Alan Powlesland, Alec Hill, Stephen Snell, Trevor Pugsley; front row: Chris Wollacott, David Jones, Brent Howard, Graham Bewes, Stephen Knight.  Squad members missing from the photo include Colin Yeo, Geoffrey Brooks, Michael Snell, Raymond Smallcombe, Stephen Wollacott.  The team went through the whole of the 1962/3 season undefeated.  (MR AND MRS A. HILL)*

*Crediton Grammar School Cadet Corps on parade in 1916. (CAHMS)*

*Crediton Grammar School Cadet Force Band, 1927.*
(*A.H. KING ROBINSON*)

*Hayward's School staff, 1955. Left to right, back row: Mr King, Mr Gore, Mr Wragge, Mr Madge, Mr Styles, Mr Hayes; front row: Mrs Webster, Mr Ash, Mr Luxton, Mr Voaden, Mrs Allard.* (*BABS STUTCHBURY*)

*The gymnasium at QES in the early years of the twentieth century. (CAHMS)*

*Shelley School as it looked when it was opened on 19 October 1962.*

*High School buildings, shortly after their construction in 1911, standing in splendid isolation.*
*(CAHMS, PHOTO BERRY)*

Above: *The south front of the Grammar School.*
*(CAHMS)*

Left: *The Victorian Landscore School building, now the 'Early Birds', a pre-school centre.*

# Chapter 10

# Inns and Hotels

Major Venn says that prior to the Dissolution (sixteenth century) there were few inns in Crediton and that most travellers would have lodged at religious houses, of which there were many at that time. This seems to be borne out by the Norden Terrier of 1598 which only shows the Angel, situated on the south side of East Street, somewhere near the junction with Charlotte Street.

Venn found records for the Angel, going back to 1504, thus confirming its antiquity. The nearest rival was the White Hart where records date from 1695, and possibly earlier if we allow for a misprint in a document which refers to the White Horse. At the time of writing the White Hart is a Cantonese restaurant called 'The Crown of Crediton'. The loss of these two ancient inns probably leaves the King's Arms on Bowden Hill as the oldest remaining in the town.

Reports of the great fire in 1743 only refer to two inns – the Lamb in North Street and the Cock near the Green. However, a map of the High Street drawn up soon after the fire indicates that there were at least 11 in that area alone, and Venn states that after the 1769 fire 13 innkeepers sued for losses. It is thought that there were up to 40 alehouses in the town around this time, although not all of them would have been inns or hotels as we recognise them today. Some would have brewed ale solely for sale and consumption off the premises.

A number of establishments closed down during the first decade of the twentieth century. They closed for a number of reasons, but it might have been partly due to concerns over the excessive consumption of alcohol that were prevalent around that time.

The name Wollacott seems to have been prominent in the pub trade in the nineteenth century, especially in the East Town. In 1822 William ran the Plymouth Inn, John the Prince, Frederick and Richard the Ring of Bells, all three establishments adjacent to the churchyard. In the middle years of the century Jane ran the Plymouth Inn and William

the Ring of Bells. In the latter part of the century William (or perhaps his son) moved to the West Town to run the Lamb in North Street. Whether these Wollacotts were related to the family who were sextons for many generations is not known.

A map of the High Street area of the town made in the eighteenth century, and depicting the town as it was before the fire of 1743, shows a number of names of inns which disappeared in that fire and possibly were never rebuilt as inns. On the north side of the High Street, just above where the Ship stands at the time of writing, there was a run of four separate establishments next door to each other. The first was the King's Head with John Warden as landlord; next was the Bear owned by Joseph Shapland; then the Red Cow owned by Capt Shepherd; and finally the Mermaid. A few doors further up the street was the Turk's Head.

There follows a very brief history of the present and many former establishments in the town.

## The Angel

Little is known of the original Angel other than that it was in East Street. The name reappeared in the High Street in the mid-eighteenth century next door but one to the Swan, with one Sam Hooker as landlord. However, by 1839 it was located at No. 18 High Street and the landlord was called James Collins. Old photographs exist showing the name of the Angel on No. 18, but it is probable that it had ceased trading as an inn by the time the pictures were taken. Indeed census records make no mention of an inn at this address after 1871. *Pigot's Directory* of 1822 gives the landlord's name as Thomas Cox, and in 1866 *Kelly's Directory* shows a Mr Partridge as the host.

## The White Hart

This was probably the second-oldest inn in the town. It took its name from the coat of arms of Richard II, who, before he became King, held the title Duke of

Exeter. The earliest record we have is a conveyance between John Northcote and Christopher Smyth in 1695, although it is reasonable to suppose there was an inn on the site much earlier, as it is located on one of the main routes into the town. The land on which the inn stands was part of the Buller estate at the beginning of the twentieth century. There have been a number of long serving and notable landlords. In the latter part of the nineteenth century the aptly named Robert Brewer was landlord for around 25 years. He was succeeded by William Burrows who was still in charge in 1935, a span of at least 35 years. In more recent times the tenant was a Mr Stanislav Tomashevski (known to all as Tom) who with his wife Joyce ran the establishment from the late 1960s for about 20 years. Tom served in the Polish navy throughout the Second World War and afterwards adopted this country as his home.

## The Crediton Inn

Often referred to as the 'Kirton Inn' it was opened in the mid-nineteenth century. Mr Badcock, the land-lord of the Horse and Jockey, objected to the licence, fearing that he would lose trade as there were already three public houses on this route through the town. The owner at the time of writing, Mrs Dianne Heggadon, is the longest-serving landlady/landlord in the town by some years, having taken over the premises in 1979.

## The Butcher's Arms Inn

This establishment had a very short life as an inn during the nineteenth century. The house is still standing in East Street and is called Vine Cottage. The reason behind the inn's name is simple: the landlord Mr John James was also a butcher. In 1864 the landlord was called Williams, and by 1870 the establishment had closed.

## The Prince Frederick

The Prince Frederick was situated on the south side of the churchyard, to the west of the main gate. It was demolished around 1836 along with a number of other buildings to make way for the construction of Union Road, and to provide extra burial space in the churchyard. The last known landlord was a John Wollacott.

It is said that the church governors wished to demolish the premises in 1810 to create extra burial space but were prevented from doing so by the terms of a bequest.

*Vine Cottage in East Street. For a short while in the middle of the nineteenth century this was the Butcher's Arms. (NORAH FOWLES)*

## The Plymouth Inn

The Plymouth Inn was situated close to the Prince Frederick and was another of the buildings demolished

*Jeanette Titt, landlady of the Plymouth Inn, at her 'retire-ment' party in 1991. At the time of writing Jeanette is still working part-time at 'Potters Bar'. Left to right: Jill Edworthy, Joan Grant, Jeanette Titt, Enid Heale, Janet Lynch, June Denford, Lill Hodge, Jane Blackburn, Mai Strong, ?. (JOAN GRANT)*

to open up Union Road. However, the name was transferred to its present site in Dean Street where it has remained ever since. One notable nineteenth-century landlord, John Stone, is said to have arranged wrestling matches in the backyard. At the height of the shoemaking industry in the town it was used as the headquarters of the Shoemaker's Guild, and around the same time was also where the Court Leet for the East Town was held until it was disbanded at the beginning of the twentieth century. In 1901 it was owned by the St Anne's Well Brewery of Exeter, and remained so until that brewery was bought out by Whitbread's in 1966.

## The Ring of Bells

This was another of the older inns in the town. It was first mentioned in 1711 in a marriage settlement between Stephen Hamlin and June Soper. (The name Hamlin appears frequently in documents referring to the ownership of inns, inferring that the family must have been fairly wealthy residents of the town.) The exact date of its closure is not certain. It was demolished to make way for the coronation memorial to George V, which was erected in 1911, but it was still standing at the funeral of General Sir Redvers Buller in 1908. It is said that the building suffered a fire at around this time and did not reopen afterwards, which may account for the uncertainty over dates.

## The Star Inn

The Star used to stand in Mill Street, not far from the junction with East Street, and would have been in a prime position to receive travellers approaching the town from the east. There is no doubt that it was old for there is a mention of the name going back as far as 1683, and if this is correct it would predate the White Hart. It was certainly an inn in 1806 when the premises were transferred from John Parnell to John Stone. It survived into the twentieth century as a public house and was then owned by Starkey, Knight & Ford of Tiverton. The name is still referred to by older Kirtonians, with the area which contains Tolleys and Mannings, often referred to as 'behind Star'.

## The Ship Hotel

The Ship was for many years the foremost licensed premises in the town. It was first mentioned in 1688 as being conveyed from John Davy to John Ivie who was lord of the manor. It still belonged to the lord of the manor at the time of the great fire of 1743, when the landlady was a Susanna Guins. However,

it has not always been on the site it is in 2004. Prior to the erection of the new market and the opening of Market Street it was sited on the other side of the High Street, almost opposite to where it now stands.

In the middle of the nineteenth century it was owned by James Williams and was often referred to as Williams' Ship Hotel. There were extensive stables and yards to the rear, including the stabling for the horses used by the fire-engine. In those times many of the town's important social functions were held at the Ship. It remained an hotel until the latter part of the twentieth century.

*The Ship Hotel, c.1925. (CAHMS)*

## The Swan Inn
## (Later The Old Swan)

The Swan was another inn that can be traced back to the time of the great fire. Throughout most of the nineteenth century it was owned by the Kenshole family. It was sold by Mr Charles Hamlin in 1906 to Mr John Moore. It closed in around 1970 and houses Ivor Coram's shoe shop in 2004.

## The Oatsheaf (Now The Exchange)

Parts of the building are said to date from the fifteenth century, and it was almost certainly called the Hare and Hounds in the eighteenth century. It was damaged by fire in 1870, and in 1906 it was sold by Charles Hamlin to Starkey, Knight & Ford. Mr W. Blatchford was the landlord in 1914 – he joined the ANZAC forces and was killed in action. It was run by Mr John Matthews and his wife for over 25 years following the Second World War. Mr Matthews also ran an undertaking business and a taxi service from the premises. For many years the rugby club used the Oatsheaf as its headquarters and changing-rooms until they obtained their own premises in the mid-1950s – for a short while after that it was used by Crediton United AFC. After Mr Matthews retired the premises were extensively altered and reopened as the Exchange.

*The Old Swan in 1906. The inn closed c.1970 and in 2004 the property is a shoe shop owned and run by Ivor Coram. (ALAN STOYLE)*

*The Oatsheaf, c.1970. (CAHMS, PHOTO FOLLAND). On 2 June 1906 Helmore's sold by auction 13 properties including the Oatsheaf, the Seven Stars and the Old Swan. The Oatsheaf was described as having a spacious light and airy bar, with a store at the rear which had formerly been used as a skittle alley, four stables and a coach-house. The premises were bought by the Tiverton brewery of Starkey, Knight & Ford. (ALAN STOYLE)*

## The Seven Stars

Yet another inn that can be traced back to the great fire, it stood next door to the Oatsheaf. In 2004, Phillips & Co., the printers and stationers. Like the two previously mentioned premises, it was sold by Charles Hamlin in 1906. In 1858 it was destroyed by fire and rebuilt. From 1874 until the beginning of the twentieth century the landlord was John Gregory who was also a builder. It closed in 1909 when the Devon Quarter Sessions refused to renew the licence.

*The Seven Stars in 1906. The inn was closed in 1909 and in 2004 the premises are owned by Phillips & Co.*
*(ALAN STOYLE)*

## The Duke of York

The Duke, sited near St Lawrence Green, was originally called the Duke William but its name was changed in the early-nineteenth century. It is likely that there was an inn on the site for many years before that. There is a reference to the Cock 'near the Green' in the account of the 1743 fire, but there is nothing to directly tie up the two names. In the early years of the twentieth century the landlady was Fanny Crosse, who had moved from the Horse and Jockey where she had previously been the landlady for 30 years. She must have been quite a formidable lady, because she was widowed at a young age and continued in the pub trade for a further 40 years.

## The Dock Inn

The Dock is the Grapevine restaurant at the time of writing. It was yet another inn to close during the twentieth century, although it did survive at least until the beginning of the First World War. One notable landlord was called Arthur Bicknell who also ran the West Town Dairy. He left the Dock to farm Chapel Downs until the outbreak of the Second World War. He was heavily involved in the town, serving as a governor of both Hayward's and the Grammar Schools, and was chairman of the Crediton branch of the NFU. He died in 1946.

*A parade preparing to set off from the Dock Inn at the Green. (PHOTO BERRY)*

## The Green Dragon

The Green Dragon stood at the entrance to St Saviours Court until the 1870s. The last landlord was called John Horrill.

## The Red Lion

Little is known about this establishment other than in the eighteenth and into the nineteenth century it was situated at the lower end of North Street.

## The Lamb

The Lamb is one of the few premises that we can be sure was standing at the time of the great fire as it is recorded that following the conflagration there was 'not a house standing in all the town, from the sign of The Lamb [in North Street] to the utmost end of The Green.' We also know that it was burnt down in the 1769 fire. The establishment was rebuilt and survived until the beginning of the twentieth century.

## The King's Arms

This is another inn which must have a long history, but little of it is known. It is said to have burnt down in a fire in the eighteenth century and been rebuilt on the same site. In times past its location would have been on the main route through the town, and it is thought that it was granted its name because some of King Charles I's troops were billeted there in 1644, during the Civil War. This almost certainly makes it the oldest building that is still a public house in the town. Recently the name has been changed to 'Kings'.

## The Market House Inn (Now The Three Little Pigs) and The Cornish Arms

The Market House and the Cornish Arms were probably two different buildings but it appears they were on or near the same location. The land was part of the Buller estate and the name 'Cornish Arms' almost certainly relates to the fact that the Buller family originated from Cornwall. The Bullers sold the property in 1912 to the Heavitree Brewery, but in 2004 it is a free house.

A new building was erected at the time of the construction of the market in the 1830s, but the name does not seem to have changed until 1851. The census held in April of that year shows Thomas Odgers as the landlord of the Cornish Arms, yet in the following month he provided a gala dinner at the Market House to celebrate the coming of the railway.

During the 1800s Charles Finch and later his son William ran a brewery in the next-door premises and almost certainly would have brewed the beer served there, and probably at a number of other establishments in the town.

In the 1950s Mr C. Way was the landlord, and at the same time he ran his transport business from the old market buildings on the opposite side of Parliament Street. In the 1970s, after the market had closed, the name was changed to the Three Little Pigs.

## The Railway Hotel

It was built in 1846 for the coming of the railway, but did not open until 1850 with Mr J. Williams as the first landlord. The railway line opened in 1851 and it was no doubt a welcome resting-place for travellers in its early days. It no longer functions as an hotel.

## The Horse and Jockey

This is another of the many inns that ceased to trade in the twentieth century. It remained open until at least 1935. In earlier times it would have been strategically placed on the main routes to North Devon and Cornwall. For many years towards the end of the nineteenth century it was run by the widow Crosse, who later went on to look after the Duke of York. It was probably a brewery as well as an inn and coach-house in past centuries as the large buildings, called 'The Maltings' in 2004, bear out. After the inn closed the pub premises were used by Edwin Tucker's as offices and the buildings behind as a grain store. At the time of writing the premises are private dwellings.

## The White Swan

The younger of the two Swans has outlived its namesake as it is still a thriving inn at the time of writing. The earliest landlord that we know of is John Wedlake in 1822. He was succeeded by John Holcombe who was landlord for around 25 years. In 1832 a baker's oven on the premises caught fire and the inn and a further dozen houses were destroyed. The inn was rebuilt as a three-storey brick building.

## No. 9 High Street (The Mitre)

In 2004 the Mitre is often referred to as No. 9. In 1901 the landlord was John Rowe who described himself as a wine and spirit merchant. His family had run the business there for many years. In 1743 the Blue Anchor stood close to the present location of the Mitre.

## The Blue Anchor

The first reference to the Blue Anchor is a conveyancing document transferring the property from John Warden to John Bridgeman in 1725. Later it was burnt down in the great fire of 1743 and suffered the same fate again in 1769. By 1780 it had been replaced by four shops in the occupation of Messrs Nott, Symes, North and Willcocks, and in 1782 Stephen Spurr paid £550 for these four shops along with the orchards and gardens lying behind 'where formerly stood the Blue Anchor'. It is thought that the premises stood at or near No. 7 High Street.

## The Royal Oak

This was possibly a new name for the Blue Anchor, for it stood next to No. 7 High Street. Also, in 1812 one Stephen Spurr is mentioned as the landlord.

Edwin Tucker's malthouse, formerly the location of the Horse and Jockey Inn. The inn sign is above the entrance. The area has since been redeveloped into dwellings and is called 'The Maltings'.

(PHOTO LUXTON)

Old Market House sign. (BABS STUTCHBURY)

A crowd awaits the Declaration of the Poll at the 1924 General Election. The White Swan is in the background. (JOHN JONES, PHOTO BERRY)

In 1876 Cornelius Hamlin bought the property and opened a bakery. It was still a baker's at the start of the First World War.

## The George or London Inn

The George changed its name to the London Inn in 1813. It stood opposite The Shambles in what was then St David's Street. *Kelly's Directory* of 1866 shows Eliza Gover as the landlady and the address as 16 High Street, which is Cox's the butchers in 2004.

## The Union Inn

The Union stood at the bottom of Deep Lane facing down Parliament Street. It was an inn for only a short time and closed in the 1860s when John Elston moved in and opened his boot and shoe factory to the rear of the premises. It was later renamed 'Oakdene'. The property was demolished some time after the Second World War.

## The Fountain

Little is known about this establishment other than that it stood at the corner of Fountain Court in 1770.

This list is by no means complete. As previously admitted there are many pub names that have long since disappeared. However, it is hoped that this information gives a flavour of the variety of establishments in the town over recent centuries.

At the time of writing the nature of the inn or public house has changed, often with the emphasis on food. Also, licensed clubs have taken some of the trade away from pubs. However, Crediton can claim to still have retained the flavour of the traditional pub in many of its remaining establishments.

*The Ring of Bells shortly before it was demolished, some time between 1908 and 1911. (MARGARET WOLLACOTT)*

# Chapter 11

# Crediton at Play

## Sport

### ASSOCIATION FOOTBALL

The earliest records of Association Football in Crediton date from the early years of the twentieth century, the first recorded side being Crediton Grammar School in the 1907/8 season.

The name Crediton United first appeared in 1910/11, but seems to have died out between the wars. After the First World War Crediton Athletic ran two teams who played at Blagdon Farm, which must have been close to the present ground at Lord's Meadow. Jackson's were also running a team at this time.

In the 1930s there seem to have been four teams in the town. Crediton Town played at the Racecourse Field at Fordton (now part of the golf course) and changed at the Railway Hotel. The other teams were Crediton Rangers, Jackson Centurions and Old Haywardians. During this period a pitch at the top of Barnfield was used on the site where the Lower (Shelley) School stands in 2004.

Crediton United was re-formed shortly after the Second World War with Bill Ash as secretary. Bill has had a long association with the club and is a past president and life member. The club played home matches at Newcombes Meadow until 1976. Teams initially used the White Hart for their changing-rooms and then took over at the Oatsheaf when the rugby club moved into their first clubhouse in the 1950s. Later the club built its own pavilion in Newcombes Meadow using part of the old Urban District Council yard. During this period they played in the Exeter and District League, but when they obtained their present headquarters and club-house at Lord's Meadow the club started to expand and widen its ambitions.

*Crediton United, c.1970. Left to right, back row: Ian Grinney (manager), John Hurst, Chris Gillard, Geoff Lee, Don Hatherley, Tim Roche, Bill Ellaway, Harry Elston, Stan Vodden;* front row: *Paul Lee, Bill Hole, Tony Elston, Dave Blanchford, Colin Hatherley, John Waldron. (CREDITON UNITED AFC)*

The first games played at Lord's Meadow were in 1976 and the social clubhouse was opened in 1979. Since then they have purchased two further pitches at Creedy Bridge to allow second, third and youth teams to play. In 1989, having outgrown the local Exeter League, the club progressed to the Western League and within three years won promotion to the Premier Division. The club struggled to compete at this level and after three seasons were relegated to the First Division. In 1998 they elected to return to play in the Devon County League. In 2004 Crediton United run eight teams, four youth and four adult.

Over the years Crediton has provided a number of players who have played professional football; mostly for Exeter City. Stan Hurst played 107 games for the club in the 1930s before transferring to Watford. Fred Davey played 276 games during the 1940s and '50s. However, pride of place must go to Keith Harvey who played almost 500 games for the club, just 12 short of the club record. Bill Ellaway and Ian Grinney also played for Exeter, Bill later going on to play for Bournemouth.

*Fordton AFC, 1959. The team was undefeated during this season, scoring 76 goals and only conceding seven.* Pictured are, left to right: *John Salter (captain), Ron Pike, Terry Eakers, George German, Alan Risden, Ian Bouget, Keith Farley, Cyril Chudley junr, Michael Eakers, Cyril Cann, Norman Bridgeman. Mr Cyril Chudley senr is being carried aloft. (*MRS A. CANN, PHOTO EXPRESS & ECHO*)*

*Crediton United (2nd XI?), 1949.* Left to right, back row: *?, Mrs Lawrence, Wally Pollard, Harold Roberts, Bill Grant, Derek Long, Perce Meldon, Johnny Robinson, Mr Stoyle, ?, ?;* front row: *Alan Grant, Scotty Radford, Jack Howard, Harry Elston, George Vicary, 'Limmy' Holmes, ? Gainey. (*MARGARET WOLLACOTT*)*

*Crediton United's captain, Bill Ellaway, being presented with the Exeter and District Senior Division 1 Cup by Mr Skinner, 1962/3 season.* Other persons pictured, left to right, are: *John Harris, Bill Ash, Norman Eakers, Ian Grinney, Jim Kenshole, Fred Davey, ?, ?, Graham Lee, Rodney Eakers, Mike Land, Chris Gillard, Dave Mills, Harry Elston.* (CREDITON UNITED AFC)

*Jackson's United Football Club, 1920–21.* Left to right, back row: *Burridge, Backwell, Discombe, ?;* middle row: *Colt, Wilkinson, Gillman;* front row: *Court, Sully, Arscott, Madge, ?.* (JOHN THEEDOM)

## CREDITON BOWLING CLUB

There may possibly have been bowling-greens in Crediton in centuries gone by, but the first record we have is of one run by Tom Metters and Arthur Richardson at the rear of the Liberal Club. This may have been the forerunner of the Crediton Bowling Club, but it was a private green purely for the use of the members of the Liberal Club and their guests.

Crediton Bowling Club was founded in 1931 and the first winner of the men's singles competition was a Mr P. Gillard. Stability has been one of the strengths of the club, for in the 73 years of its existence it has had only 13 secretaries. The longest serving were Tom Metters from 1933 to 1956, J.E. Taylor from 1959 to 1966 and Tony Bond from 1989 to 2000. Also, Karen Theedom has been treasurer since 1987 and is still in post in 2004.

The small wooden hut that serves as a clubhouse has been expanded four times over the years and is a structure of which the club can be proud. One of the club's longest-serving members, Don Durrant, supervised the first extension. Don was well known for his fund-raising ability and he even managed to persuade one of the teachers from Exeter Technical College to send some apprentices on day-release to Crediton to undertake the work as a project.

The club had rather humble beginnings, and during its lifetime has struggled for members. At one time during the 1960s there were just 20 male members and three ladies. Indeed, for a while the ladies' section folded altogether, before re-forming in 1980. Ron Joslin remembers that it was often the same 16 who would represent the the club in both matches and friendlies, and that you could not afford to be ill during the season for fear of letting the club down.

The fortunes of the club have certainly changed since those days. At the time of writing the club has around 100 members. Crediton's club, both the men's and women's sections, is now one of the most respected in the county. The club achieved its first major honour in 1988, winning the County Fours. In the same year father and son John and Mark Theedom won the Devon under-40s pairs.

In 1974 Don Durrant became the first member to represent the county. He was followed by his son David. Since then many others have earned that honour. The ladies have also earned many honours since 1980, most recently Christine Theedom and Ruth Bond won the ladies' over-55 competition in 2002.

The Bond family have been associated with the club for much of its life. Tony Bond, who died in 2002, was Devon President in 1999, his wife Ruth and sons Chris and Ian are all members at the time of writing. Ian is one of two international bowlers that the club can boast. Although both Ian and Simon Stevens are indoor internationals and play out of the Exonia Club in Exeter, but they both learnt the game at Crediton and still play for the club in the summer.

Ian Bond has gained an international reputation as an indoor bowler with a long list of honours, his most noted achievement being winning the televised BUPA open tournament in 2002. He also won the Scottish open in 2003.

*Crediton Bowling Club, c.1933, shortly after the club was opened.*
(*CREDITON BOWLING CLUB, WESTERN TIMES*)

*Crediton Bowling Club, ladies interclub winners of 1992. Left to right, back row: Eileen Rich, Joan Martin, Liz Grey, Dorothy Richards, Ruth Bond; front row: Christine Theedom, Cynthia Bishop (captain), Sybil Way. These ladies formed the backbone of the ladies section during its years of success in the 1980s and '90s. (CREDITON BOWLING CLUB)*

*The White Hart team, winners of the Industrial Bowls Tournament in 1989. Left to right: Colin Fribbens, Dave Robbins, Jill Medcraft, Kevin Richards.*

*Crediton Bowling Club, trophy winners of 1959. Left to right: Mr Braund, Tom Gainey, Tony Bond, ?, Roy Whieldon, Tom Metters, Don Durrant, George Moore, Bill Stidder.*

*(CREDITON BOWLING CLUB, PHOTO AUTHERS)*

## CREDITON CRICKET CLUB

Crediton Cricket Club was formed in 1864 and the last fixtures for which records survive were in 1968, so it lasted for over 100 years. It is believed that throughout its existence the club played its home games at the Exhibition Field. For most of this time Crediton would have shared the pitches with Queen Elizabeth School. The majority of the club's home matches were played on a Sunday as the school used the wicket on Saturdays during term time, however, once the school had broken up for the summer holidays the wicket was available for the use of the town team on Saturday afternoons.

Cricket continued to be played on the Exhibition Road square for some years after 1968 with friendly matches mainly taking place of an evening between 'pub' and 'company' teams. An artificial strip was laid during the 1980s, but unfortunately fell into disrepair, and sadly in 2004 virtually no cricket is played on a ground that was once considered to be one of the best batting wickets in Devon.

The 1905 season appears to have been particularly good for batsmen. On 2 August Sir J.F. Shelley scored 200 not out against Exeter, and two weeks later, on 19 August, J. Symes scored 203 when Crediton beat Shobrooke by scoring 281 for the loss of two wickets against their total of 64.

During the 1950s the town had a strong side and they twice won the Sim Cup, a competition consisting of two 22-overs-per-side matches played on consecutive days; the winner being the team scoring the most aggregate runs over the two matches. The 1956 final against Whipton, played at the county ground in Exeter on 12 and 13 July, must have been a very exciting affair as Crediton won the match by just three runs. For those interested in statistics, Whipton batted first in the first match and scored 78 for the loss of nine wickets, in reply Crediton scored 103 for eight. Crediton batted first in the second match and scored an impressive 138 for four in their 22 overs and must have thought they were home and dry. However, Whipton amassed 160 for four, almost depriving Crediton of victory. Apparently on the team's return to Crediton the celebrations went on well into the early hours of the following morning.

A report on the 1959 season has come to light and reads as follows:

*It was a wonderful summer for cricket with good wickets, although we as a team did not score enough runs to avoid defeat in several games, only one batsman (Billy Mustard) scored over the sixties, although six others got their fifties. Our two opening bowlers, Fred Davey and Brian Lock, collected over sixty wickets apiece. We were pleased to see Philip Tait and Richard Best, two youngsters who also bowl extremely well. We also held double the catches from the season before. Nets will commence every Tuesday and Thursday evening at 7 p.m., from April 19th, 1960.*

*Match Results*

*Played 35 Won 16 Drawn 8 Lost 11
Cancelled 3, Rain Stopped Play 1.*

*Crediton Cricket Club centenary match, Crediton versus President's XI, June 1964. Left to right, back row: Henry Pinfold, Colin Beer, Keith Harvey, David Brough, David Tucker, Graham Lee, Bob Cope, A. Robinson, Robin Langhorne, Mike Wadey, E. Davenport, N. Giles or L. Martland, Geoff Saltmarsh, Ray Mason, Ted Powlesland;* middle row: *Tony Bond, Bill Ellaway, Ian Grinney, David Shepherd, John Roach, Clifford Wadey, Maurice Setters, Fred Davey;* front row: *Paul Radnor, Alan Tonkin, Joe Sherwood, Bill Mustard, Bill Colling, N. Giles or L. Martland.*

*Crediton Cricket Club, 1896.* Left to right, standing: *A.C. Durant, J. Symes, C.G. Lovesey, G.G. Orme, D.H. Tothill, ?;* seated: *M. Steed, E.F.P. Jones, R. Knight, A. Churcher, A.J. Powlesland;* on ground: *G. Llewellin, A.W. Badcock.* (Mrs Jean Roach)

*Crediton Congregational Church Cricket Team, 1952. On the day this picture was taken they beat Torquay Congregationalists by 50 runs. Left to right, back row: Revd G. Williams, Keith Harvey, Denis Williams, John Wilson, Den Clarke, Stan Hurst; front row: Tony Holloway, Cyril Wollacott, Billy Duffy, Clifford Wilcox, Wilf Hunt.*

*(CAHMS)*

*Crediton Cricket Club – the Sim Cup winning team of 1956. Left to right, back row: ?, R.H. (Bob) Cope, Bill Ellaway, Ian Grinney; front row: Brian Nokes, Keith Harvey, Ted Powlesland, Brian Lock, Fred Davey, John Roach, Bill Colling. (Mrs Jean Roach)*

*A record partnership, 16 July 1955. Bill Colling (left) was out for 87 off the last ball of the innings. John Roach scored 119 not out. The opponents were Bradninch who, at close of play, were 143 for 6. The match was, therefore, a draw. (Mrs Jean Roach)*

## GOLF IN CREDITON

The Crediton and District Golf Club was formed on 23 November 1923. A total of 125 shares of £5 were issued and there were 66 shareholders, nearly all of whom were prominent local business and professional persons. The professional was Mr A. Whittaker, who was paid £1 per week retainer, and the greenkeeper was Mr Bert Jasper. In 1935 the secretary was Mr W. Copp, whose son is a member of the new club in 2004. It was a nine-hole course located near the River Yeo between Fordton and Uton, but no trace of its existence remains.

The club thrived in the early days and by 1932 the membership stood at 125, with the annual subscription being £2. The course remained open throughout the Second World War when, according to Mr F.G. Bourne who wrote to the *Crediton County Courier* in 1976, the fairways were obstructed to stop any enemy aircraft landing on the site.

After the war the club began to suffer financial problems, mainly caused by falling membership. In 1948 it made a loss and the landlord demanded increased rent, and there was an urgent need to renew ancient and worn-out course-maintenance machinery. The then secretary, Jan Ridd, made an urgent appeal for more money, but by the Annual General Meeting held on 13 April 1949 insufficient extra funds had been raised. A further appeal was made without success and on 2 May, with the membership standing at 36 men, 12 ladies and two juniors, a decision was made to close the club.

On 4 April 1951 a sale was conducted by Helmores. The clubhouse was sold to Mr H. Dart of Coldridge, to be used as a deep-litter hut, and the other house was sold to Okehampton Rifle Club. The sale realised £407; a sad and rather undignified end.

Two decades had passed when, in October 1972, a group of golf enthusiasts got together to try to form a new club. Bert Egmore, who was agent for the Downes estate, saw the opportunity of providing land for a course. He approached Alan Swann, who in turn sounded out other potential interested parties. A steering committee was formed consisting of Les Evans, Harold Martin, Les Pope, Alan Rodd, Colin Smith and Jim Madge, with Alan Swann as chairman and the venture was under way. Captain M.F. Buller, the owner of the land, agreed a long-term lease on favourable terms and work on the course and conversion of the two Victorian cottages began.

On 19 April 1975 the clubhouse and a temporary nine-hole course was opened by Lt Col T.D. Brown, the president of the Devon Golf Union. Just over 12 months later, on 13 June 1976, at the beginning of one of the hottest and driest summers for years, the course was officially opened by Michael Barratt (at that time a celebrity, as presenter of Nationwide). The opening was celebrated with an exhibition match with players including Neil Coles and Tommy Horton, both of whom were at the time top players on the European Tour.

Since then the club has grown in stature and the course has matured into one of the best in the county. In 2004 it has over 700 members.

*Downes Crediton Golf Club. The steering committee are pictured sitting on a mound behind the 18th green shortly after the club opened in 1976.* Left to right: *Alan Rodd, Bert Egmore, Alan Swann (chairman), Harold Martin, W.L. Evans.*
(DOWNES CREDITON GOLF CLUB, PHOTO LES ASHPLANT)

Above: *The clubhouse, Downes Crediton Golf Club, before conversion. The mound of grass in the foreground is now the site of the ninth green.* (PHOTO LES ASHPLANT)

Right: *Ian Harris, winner of both senior and junior club championships in 1993, the only time this feat has been achieved.* (MARGARET TUCKER)

## CREDITON RFC – A BRIEF HISTORY
### By Paul Harris

The origin of the game of rugby, in the context of William Webb Ellis' contribution, is a much-debated issue. However, from a Crediton perspective there is little doubt that rugby in the town was initially inspired by the Grammar School in the mid-1870s, enthusiastically organised by Charles George Lovesey who, over the next 25 years, became one of the most respected players and administrators in the county.

As the game evolved in the town, the latter part of the nineteenth century saw such a growth in the game that at one time there were as many as six different teams playing in the town. The Crediton club, although officially accepted as being formed in 1878, actually played fixtures in early 1877, and the team comprised Grammar School boys, masters and local interested individuals. It was not until 1882 that the club as we know it at the time of writing was actually formed.

In 1895–96 it is understood that five clubs within the town (the Crediton Town Club, Crediton Juniors, Crediton Scarlet Runners, Crediton Rovers and Crediton Dark Blues) decided to amalgamate and a change to the club colours, from black and yellow to light blue and brick-red hoops, would support that idea.

Success followed and in 1898 Crediton won the Devon Senior Cup for the first and, so far, only time. Many players had represented the county; indeed Crediton at the time was one of the leading clubs in Devon. The club reverted to its original colours of black with a yellow sash in 1899.

Interest in the game waned for a period up to the outbreak of the First World War, due in the main to the rise of Association Football as well as the controversies which surrounded the playing of Northern Rules (Rugby League as we now know it), whereby players would be either compensated for loss of income or blatantly paid for playing.

Between the wars, once again, Crediton developed into a fine side, although by this period was regarded as a junior club. The 1920s brought much success to the club, reaching the final of the Devon Junior Cup on a number of occasions before winning it in 1924. This feat was not repeated until 1947 when Buckfastleigh were defeated in the final.

The club really began to develop in the mid-1950s when, after using the Oatsheaf pub (now the Exchange) as its headquarters for almost 75 years, funds were raised to purchase the old fire station on the recreation-ground in Exhibition Road. With the ability to generate income through the bar and social functions, the club thrived. Some 12 years later, the ground used at the time of writing was purchased and the clubhouse and changing-rooms built. The clubhouse was extended in the 1970s with the addition of a lounge bar and improvements to the kitchen and dining areas. The grandstand was also erected to provide sheltered seating for up to 150 people.

The 1980s saw the emergence of a wonderful youth section which is still flourishing in 2004. Hundreds of young players have come through the youth system and played at senior level for the club, and many have progressed further to play at a higher level. The introduction of leagues in 1987 saw Crediton become the first winners of the Cornwall and Devon league and, although fortunes have fluctuated since then, in 2004 the team plays at the highest level that it has ever achieved in the South West 1 league.

*Crediton Rugby Football Club, 1946–47, winners of the Devon Junior Cup. Crediton beat Buckfastleigh by three points to nil in the final at the county ground.* Left to right, standing: *T. Farley, E.J.R. Bidgood, E. Boddy, A. Heard, L. Wollacott, D. Trick, W.G. Lee, D. Heard, A. King Robinson, T. Cullis, F.J. Steer, L. Turner, W. Heard, H. Blaen, L. Stockman, A. Boddy;* middle row: *A. Labbett, D. Cornall, W. Lee, E. Powlesland, R. Turner, D. Prettejohns, T. Fennessy;* front row: *F. Tuckett, L. Boddy, C. Haydon, N. Littlejohns. (Paul Harris)*

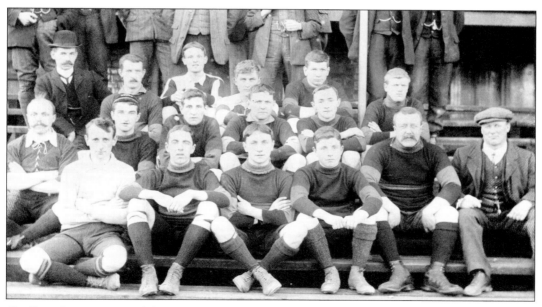

*Crediton Conservative Club Rugby Team, 1907. They had just beaten St Thomas by one try to nil at the county ground. (CAHMS)*

# *Crediton's International Sportsmen and Women*

*Ian Bond pictured holding a replica of the 2001 World Bowls Tour Players Trophy. He was first capped as an indoor bowler in 1991 at the age of 17 and has been an international ever since. At the start of 2004 he was ranked sixth in the world. His first major trophy was the national single title in 1995. In 2002 he won the BUPA International Open and was a semi-finalist in the World Championships. In December 2003 he won the Scottish Open.* (CREDITON COUNTRY COURIER)

*Alex Perry, table-tennis international, c.2000. First capped in 1994, he is still in the England team. Alex also played in the Swedish National League.*

(MARGARET TUCKER)

*Becky Brooks, Tae Kwon Do international, c.2003. She is a former World Under-18 Champion and in 2003 she finished fourth in the World Championships in Miami – she has been English Champion three times. Tae Kwon Do has over 35,000 active participants in the UK. Becky is making a career out of teaching the art, and has already attracted a number of other international participants to her classes and seminars held in Crediton.*

*Simon Stevens, international bowler, spring 2004. Simon plays outdoor bowls for Crediton, but represents Exonia when playing indoor bowls. He qualified for the Indoor World Championships in 2004.*

(CREDITON COUNTRY COURIER)

## CREDITON DARTS LEAGUE

The Crediton Darts League was formed in 1947, but the game must have been played in Crediton's pubs and clubs for generations before that, although apparently not on an organised basis. The number of licensed premises providing teams for the league has fallen off since the days of the 1950s and '60s when just about every 'house' in the town and surrounding area had a team. Indeed, today many pubs don't even have a board. The game certainly did seem to be in decline for a time in the 1970s, but since the mid-1980s it seems to have settled at a league of around 16 teams.

The type of game has changed over the years. In the early days a league match consisted of ten best-of-three legs games of 201, double start and finish. At a date in around 1980 the format was changed to nine games of 301. In 1985 a further change took place when six games of singles and three of pairs were introduced. This is still the format played in 2004.

The Ladies Darts League was formed in 1972. In 2004 it has two divisions and matches consist of five singles games and two pairs of 301.

*Crediton Inn ladies' darts team, first winners of the Sleet Cup in 1972. The cup is awarded in memorial to Mrs Sleet who was instrumental in founding the ladies league, but died before the first season was complete. Her husband, Harry Sleet, is on the far left of the picture having presented the trophy.* Others pictured, from left to right, are: *Pam Eakers, Joan Grant, Miss Sleet, Phyllis Gale, Stella Jones, June Bilcock, Flo Weedon.* (PHYLLIS WALTERS)

*Presentation of darts trophies, c.1964, by Mr J. Taylor to Roy Edwards. Len Hunt, landlord of the Duke of York, and Den Edwards are looking on.*

(CAHMS, PHOTO FOLLAND)

## CREDITON SKITTLES LEAGUE

Skittles is an ancient pub game and in centuries gone by most inns and coach-houses would have had an alley, usually situated in a barn or an outhouse. Deeds for establishments such as the Seven Stars, which closed almost 100 years ago, mention a skittle alley as part of the premises.

There is no doubt that the game was played in the town in times gone by, but organised skittles only started in the 1960s. At that time the Liberal Club had the only alley, and when ten teams formed the initial league all matches were played there. Players that remember those early days say that most games were played on a Friday, as the room was required for bingo on other days. Also, teams would only play one or two games a month. Information about the early years of the league has been difficult to come by, because records do not appear to have survived from those days. Among the first teams to form the original league were the Liberal Club, two teams from the White Hart and a

team from Bow. In the early years a group broke away from the Liberal Club side and called themselves the Nomads; this team is still playing in the league in 2004. The next pub to open an alley was the King's Arms, later followed by the White Swan and the Railway Hotel. At the time of writing over 20 establishments in Crediton and the surrounding villages have their own alleys and support around 40 teams who play in a league of three divisions. Most matches are played on a Monday or Tuesday during the winter months.

Harry Barnes of the Liberal Club was instrumental in setting up the league and was chairman for many years. Di Perry, who at the time of writing has been secretary for approaching 20 years, still runs the league with Phil Bevan as chairman. In the 1970s and '80s skittles finals night, which was held at the Queen Elizabeth Lower School, was one of the social highlights of the year, often with a TV celebrity on hand to give out the prizes. Unfortunately, in 2004, finals night is a much smaller and less well supported affair, but the league itself is still in a very healthy state.

*Ernie's Fliers skittle team, 1977/8. The team swept the board, winning all trophies. This photograph was taken outside Crediton Bowling Club later in the year.* Left to right: *Ernie Steer, Ron Joslin, Aubrey Board, Tom Richards, Eric Pike, Harry Elston, Mark Theedom, Ken Hooper.* (CREDITON COUNTRY COURIER)

*'Follies', winners of the skittles league in 1983/4 and 1985/6.* Left to right: *Owen Rich, Gordon Shrubsole, Brian Courts, Norman Morrish, Phil Smith, Colin Fribbens, Glenis Fribbens, Andy Burridge* (hidden), *Carl Shore Marston, Chris Courts.*

# Crediton Carnival

It is impossible to say exactly when Crediton Carnival started, indeed it is likely that it grew out of one of the annual fairs in the town, but we do have a photographic record going back virtually 100 years. One of the oldest photographs shows a 'black and white' minstrel troupe – a tradition that was continued until just before the Second World War.

For over 100 years, Crediton Rugby Club had organised the carnival, but in 1994 they decided to hand over the reigns to someone else. A group called the Mid Devon Carnival Circuit Committee ran the event until 1997, when the Crediton Lions Club took over. The latter organisation has run it ever since. The Lions Club have approached the task with great enthusiasm despite waning interest in the town, although they have said that 2004 will be their last year. In addition to events in Carnival Week they have also organised a summer quiz competition which has added to the money raised for local charities. Crediton is fortunate still to have its carnival, because, faced with increased costs and lack of interest, many other towns and cities much larger than Crediton have lost their annual carnival in the early-twenty-first century.

The route for the carnival has changed over the years. It would appear that before the Second World War the parade met at the railway station. In 1938 the *Express and Echo* reported that the torchlit procession was both 'picturesque and colourful'. However, there was a problem, for the article continued:

*As the procession was about to move off... the oil saturated wick of a torchlight exploded out on to the thatch roof of the tableau exhibited by Messrs Walton's of Exeter... several men ran forward and after frantically beating the flames with hands and sticks, managed to extinguish them before any damage could be done.*

In the 1950s the parade started from Western Road, processed down the town as far as the White Hart and then returned via Park Street and Union Terrace. This had to be changed when it was realised that the weight of the vehicles was potentially too heavy to go down Union Terrace (the Lynch). At the time of writing the procession starts from the industrial estate, going up the High Street into St Saviours Way, along Greenway and returning down the High Street.

It is a tradition that the final float in the evening procession has been a 'last appeal'. For many years 'Gifty' Steer made this position his own; in 2003 the task was shared by Peter Howison and Alan Tonkin. Both have associations with the rugby club, so the club has not completely lost touch with the organisation of the carnival.

*Crowning of Crediton Carnival Queen, 1971. Left to right, standing: Alan Tonkin, Mary Blamey, Len Boddy;* seated: *Stephen Smith, Julie Neiass, Gillian Wright, Elaine Champion, Greta Phillips. (CAHMS, PHOTO FOLLAND)*

*Crediton Minstrel Troupe, at the carnival in 1909. Included in the picture are: Elias Elston (left, back row), Charles Cann and Fred Elston (second row from back), F.J. Helmore (left, front row), 'Buckie' Forward (seated).*

(CAHMS)

*Crediton Carnival (possibly 1908). These are entrants for the children's fancy-dress parade.*
(CAHMS, PHOTO BERRY)

*A postcard dating from the beginning of the twentieth century depicting Crediton Red Cross Choir outside the King's Arms on Carnival Day. The writing on the postcard states: 'This is the party that was at the sideshow next door just ready to start off in the railway van. They went to Downes, Lady Audrey was so pleased with their performance gave them a sovereign so that was a real help up'. (PLIMSOLE COLLECTION)*

*Crediton Guides and Brownies Pantomime, c.1960. The Andy Pandys and Teddies are,* left to right, back row: *Margaret Avery, Brenda Mason, Fiona Gale, Janet Chant, Heather Cole, Virginia ?;* front row: *Susan Brealey, Susan Batters, Linda Batters, Christine Courtney, Lyn Tonkins, Annette Boucher.*

*(MARGARET SANDERCOCK, PHOTO AUTHERS)*

*Crowning of the Crediton Carnival Queen in 1988. Left to right: Nina Osborne, Jenny Robbins, Janet Hopper, Mrs Gillian Ponsford (chairman of Crediton Town Council), Stephanie Jewell (front) with Katrina Bayley, the 1987 Carnival Queen (behind). Janet was also Carnival Queen in 1983 and 1989. (CREDITON COUNTRY COURIER)*

Above: *The amazing dancing bear, c.1910. (CAHMS, PHOTO BERRY)*

Left: *Crediton Carnival, 1950 – Palace of the Snow Queen. Left to right, back row: ?, Margaret Tuckett, ?; centre: Tim Roche; front row: Julie Elson, Pam Wheeler. (CAHMS)*

## Crediton Cinema

The Palace Cinema in East Street was opened in 1933. It was originally owned by Mr Freddie Authers who built it over part of the site of his sweet factory. Prior to that films had been shown at the Town Hall. It survived as a cinema for just 40 years. For the second half of that period Henry Wotton was the manager. In the late in 1960s it closed for the first time, but reopened under the name of the Regal for a short period before closing again in the 1970s. It then opened again, this time as a bingo hall under the name of the 'Crown Bingo and Social Club', but that did not survive for long either.

In 1984 the building was purchased by John Gregory and Ian Street with the intention of opening it as a nightclub. This project met with a great deal of local opposition and the idea was dropped in favour of a snooker club. 'Crediton Snooker Club' opened in 1986, and in 1989 its name was changed to 'Potters Bar'. The business was sold in 2001 and in 2004 is owned by Clive Gorrett, Nigel Kelly and Sam Knight.

The club has always been active in local sports and has teams in the Exeter Snooker League, Crediton and Devon Pool leagues and Crediton Darts leagues. In David Williams it can boast an England international pool player.

Above: *Cinema bill poster, 1937.* (BABS STUTCHBURY)

Below: *Programme of films at the Palace Cinema, July 1957.* (CAHMS)

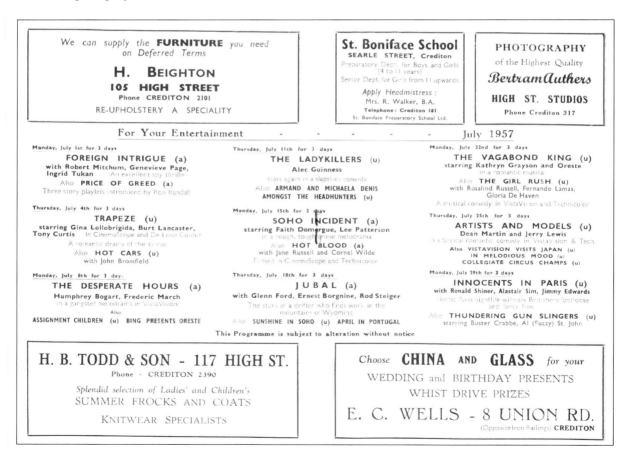

*The Palace Cinema, East Street.* (PHOTO AUTHERS)

## Crediton Women's Institute

On Monday 2 December 1946 a public meeting was held with a view to starting a branch of the Women's Institute in Crediton. Mrs Bruce Adams was elected the first president, and Lady Lennard and Mrs Harry vice-presidents. In the early days meetings were held at Newcombes on the third Wednesday in the month between 7p.m. and 9p.m. They consisted of a short business meeting followed by a social evening and judging of the competition for the month. The first competition was for the 'best woollen darn' and the prize was shared between Lady Lennard and Miss Kirkland. Meetings always commenced with the singing of 'Jerusalem' and closed with the National Anthem. Within a couple of years of opening attendance at meetings was regularly around the 60 mark, and it was decided that a woman had to be over 18 years of age before she could become a member. In the 1960s the organisation used the Church Workers Institute and in the 1970s moved just a few doors away to the Masonic Hall.

In later years speakers and presentations were a regular feature on the agenda. For example, in 1967 the members were given a demonstration of the wonders of the latest technology, 'the Kenwood Mixer'. However, more serious topics were also dealt with, for in that same year Dr Margaret Jackson gave an illustrated talk about her recent trip to India and the poverty she had witnessed there. In 1969 the members were given a tour of the West of England School for the Deaf to see the work that organisation carried out.

Crediton Women's Institute is still flourishing at the time of writing, but like most organisations membership levels are not what they were 50 years ago. In 2004 membership stands in the mid-30s, and under-18s would now be welcomed.

*'It's not all Jam and Jerusalem'. Members of Crediton WI at their annual party in 1984, held at Flaire Club. Pictured here, left to right: Dorothy Sanderson, Sylvia Heaton, Edith Kirkham, Mrs Jamieson, Joy Deverall, Mrs Silverson, Vera Ashton.*

(CREDITON WI)

## –·· PROGRAMME ···–

### MEETINGS 7—9 P.M. THIRD WEDNESDAY OF THE MONTH

**January 21st.** Miss Williams, M.A.—Education in U.S.A.

Competition: Covered Coathanger.

**February 18th.** Health Talk—E. M. Johnston, B.A.—Nature Cure.

Competition: Printers' Errors.

**March 18th.** British Railways—Travel Films.

Competition: 6 Biscuits—either Ginger, Easter or Savoury.

**April 13th.** Group Meeting.

**April 15th.** Sergeant Taylor—Duties of a Policewoman.

Competition: Safety-first Limerick.

**May 20th.** Members' Night.

**June 17th.** Mrs. Bailey—Floral Arrangement.

Competition: Arrangement of Wild Flowers in anything but a vase.

**July 15th.** Doctor Sawyers.

Competition: A Gift of Fruit for an invalid.

**September 16th.** Mrs. Lockyear—Foundation Garments.

Competition: A Hot Water Bottle Cover.

**October 21st.** Miss Primmer—Growing Pot Plants indoors.

Competition: A Pot Plant.

**November 18th.** Annual Meeting. V.C.O.

Competition: A Hand-made Toy.

**December 9th.** S.W. Electricity Co.—Cookery Demonstration—Biscuits, Sweet and Savoury.

Competition: Cake Competition.

### TRADING STALL AT EACH MEETING

*The WI programme for 1959.* (CREDITON WI)

*Crediton Townswomen's Guild. The presentation of Long-Service Awards, July 2000.* Left to right: *Vera Hurst, Pam Durrant (chairman), Mary Knight (Federation chairman), Norah Fowles, Rose Roberts. The Crediton Townswomen's Guild was founded in 1967. Over 40 women attended the first meeting in March of that year and the organisation prospered in the town until, at its peak, there were around 90 members. In recent years interest has waned and in 2004 membership is around the 30 mark. The purpose of the organisation, which grew out of the suffragette movement, is to fight for better educational, professional and creative opportunities for women. In the early days the Crediton branch held its meetings at the youth centre in the former Hayward's School buildings. Later they moved to the Masonic Hall.* (MRS YVONNE GREEN)

*Crediton Fair in the High Street, 1910.* (PHOTO BERRY)

*Pat Henson as Dick and Margaret Campbell as Tommy the Cat in* Dick Whittington. *Girl Guides and Brownies pantomime, 1958/59.*

(MARGARET SANDERCOCK,
PHOTO AUTHERS)

*The Gang Show, c.1960. Bert White, as presiding judge, is pictured, flanked on his left by Den Turner and George Stookes, and on his right Douglas Penny and Terry Stoneman.* (DAVID WHITE, PHOTO AUTHERS)

*Work is completed on the 50th anniversary Scout Memorial Garden in Peoples Park in 1957. Left to right, back row: Ron Coombes, George Stookes, Charlie Ford, Ron Avery; front row: Harry Branton, Bert White, Tom White, Bill Lake.* (DAVID WHITE)

# The Town Band

The Town Band can trace its origins back to the middle of the nineteenth century and it is quite possible that it functioned before then. For most of the interwar period it was headquartered at the King's Arms and used the inn for practice. In those days the bandmaster was Mr J. Bennellick.

It was subsidised by a small grant from the Urban District Council and in return the band was required to play at a certain number of events each year. They gave regular concerts in Newcombes Meadow roughly where the St Boniface Statue stands in 2004. In the 1930s there were rows of wooden seats built into the hillside. Ron Hamlin remembers that it was a very cold spot, and some evenings they would play to an audience that consisted purely of one or two friends and relatives of the band. They also used to play in the High Street and each year lead the carnival and Armistice Day processions.

In 1950 players started to go to other bands, and there was bad feeling among the members. The minutes for a meeting in 1954 record that:

*The bandmaster Mr S.W. Setter thanked the Band for their support in the past and expressed the hope for renewed enthusiasm and full practices in the future. Without good practices the Band can do nothing, with such a small party we must be all in.*

In fact the band continued until 1963 but with very limited support.

The re-formed band grew from the Crediton Community Play of 1983. A group played Christmas carols in the High Street that year, but it was not until March 1984 that the band started up again officially. For the first year of their existence they were called the Crediton Community Band, but soon reverted to the title of Town Band. They played on instruments borrowed from the South Molton Band, and relied heavily on four players who came from Lympstone to get them going. Also, Wilson Forster was a major driving-force both on the playing side as well as fund-raising. Within two years they had raised enough money to buy their own instruments and uniforms. Ron Hamlin, one of the members of the original band, had salvaged many of the old instruments which stood the new band in good stead in the early years. Indeed the bass drum used to this day is the original.

At the time of writing the band travels far and wide to give concerts, and in the summer of 2004 made their third visit to Dokkum in Holland. The Dokkum Oranje Band has also visited Crediton, the first time in 1988. Concerts have been held at Blenheim Palace, the Millennium Dome and Longleat.

The only marching duty the band undertakes is for the Remembrance Day parade, otherwise almost all events are concerts, as well as playing in the High Street on carnival day and before Christmas.

Ron Hamlin joined the band as a young man in the early 1930s, but sadly died at the age of 90 in April 2004. He was still playing the same 'B-flat bass' only a few weeks before he died, which he started with when he joined the band. He believed that the instrument may have been older than him.

*Crediton Town Band in 1922 outside the King's Arms.* Left to right, back row: *H. Setter, G. Pike, L. Lynes;* middle row: *R. Westcott, W. Harvey, H. Grant, R. Sprague, F. Harvey, A. Eales, T. Ralph;* front row: *H. Cornall, W. Burridge, T. Carruthers, J. Bennellick, A. Setter, C. Mogridge, F. Hill. (CAHMS)*

*The late Ron Hamlin with his 'B-flat bass' and the bass drum donated by William Jackson. This drum is still used by the band in 2004. (RON HAMLIN)*

*Crediton Town Band, 1985, shortly after the band was re-formed.* Left to right, back row: *Deborah Arscott, Sarah Hayley, Lisa Marklew, Janice Gutens, Jason Keen, Dean Morgan, Bill Stoneman;* middle row: *Nicola Arscott, Mel Hansford, Eddy Popham, Ted Everit, Diane Hill, Ian Heard, Jack Heard;* front row: *Arthur Arscott, Toby Cushion, Ron Howard, Wilson Forster, Keith Phillips, Ron Hamlin, Terry Ham.*

(ARTHUR ARSCOTT)

*The Cheese Club, based at the White Swan, raises money for local charities. Here, John Davey, chairman of the club, is seen presenting a cheque to Francesca Raymont of Crediton Churches Holiday Club which organises entertainment for children between the ages of 5 and 11 during the school holidays. On the left is Bob Seymour (Cheese Club secretary) and standing behind is club member Bill Davey.* (CREDITON COUNTRY COURIER)

## Crediton Operatic and Dramatic Society

Crediton Operatic Society, as it was first known, was formed in April 1964 and its opening production, *HMS Pinafore* by Gilbert and Sullivan, took place the following spring. The ladies made their own dresses and bonnets while the sailors' uniforms were war surplus tropical whites from Rawle, Gammon & Baker in Exeter. The officers' uniforms were borrowed from ex-naval personnel. The first four productions were Gilbert and Sullivan works, but the society broke with this tradition in 1969 with a performance of 'Merrie England' by Edward German.

In the early years of COS the musical accompaniment was provided by two pianists. Eventually, an orchestra was formed of local musicians for each production, not only consisting of a full line-up of instruments but sometimes of just a small group of keyboard, guitars, bass and drum, depending on the requirements of the show in question.

In 1972 COS became CODS with the introduction of the drama section, the first play being *The Chalk Garden*. Since then productions have ranged from murder mysteries to comedies taking in works by playwrights such as Alan Ayckbourn, Noel Coward and Agatha Christie. Soon afterwards the choral section was also developed. Their performances have included Viennese and American evenings and a 'Best of British' production.

Over the years CODS has evolved and tried to move with the times. In 1999 the society gave a performance of *Fiddler on the Roof* and in 2001 they performed a contemporary work, *The Hired Man* by Melvyn Bragg and Howard Goodall. The 2002 operatic performance was an ambitious production of *Carmen* which proved a great success. In recent years productions have been performed 'in the round', which proved rather unnerving for the majority of the cast at first.

An organisation such as CODS is always very reliant on its 'backstage' members for scenery, lighting, costume, etc. Costuming a show is often one of the more difficult tasks as not all hired items come in the correct sizes. For example, bridesmaids dresses for the 1974 production of *Ruddigore* that were supposed to be size 12 when unpacked were found to fit a 44-inch bust! Hasty alterations had to be made.

At the time of writing CODS performs two major productions each year. In the spring it is a musical production and in the autumn a play. The choral group also perform one major production each autumn and a number of smaller performances in local halls or private premises.

CODS is a vibrant and progressive group which will celebrate its 40th anniversary in 2005. Over the years it has not been afraid to take on a challenge and because of this it has won a number of National Operatic and Dramatic Association Awards for excellence in amateur theatre in the South West.

*The cast of the CODS's first production* HMS Pinafore *in 1965. The leading roles were taken by Ashley Williams, Ronald Cairns, Bill Lee, Clifford Wadey, Julian Redfern, Martin Wreford, Paul Roberts, Brenda Law, Freddie Kaye and Shirley Sims. The producer was Anthony Staden and the musical director was Dorothy Sheppard. (CODS)*

*Chapter 12*

# Transport

## Road Transport

For centuries farmers and merchants would have brought their goods to Crediton market by pack-horse as the roads, such as they were, were virtually impassable by any form of wheeled vehicle, especially in winter. Horse- and ox-drawn carts were used but sledges which could be dragged over the mud would probably have been more common.

Travel by road over any distance would have been difficult. We read of men such as Charles Wesley, who, 300 years ago, travelled widely around the West Country on horseback, preferring to be at the mercy of the elements, rather than in a covered carriage. In those times progress by horseback would probably have been quicker and more comfortable than in a rough carriage, with wooden wheels and almost certainly no springs.

Until an Act of Parliament was passed during the reign of Queen Elizabeth I (1558–1603), local parishes were responsible for the upkeep of roads and many did little or nothing to towards this. It was not until the introduction of the turnpike road that any real improvement could be seen. Prior to this the journey from Exeter to London took 3½ days in summer and six days in winter. By the early-nineteenth century this had been reduced to 17 hours.

Devon was late to introduce the turnpike. The first roads did not come until 1750, some 50 years after the rest of the country. According to William Pope the original turnpikes through Crediton went past the White Hart, through Mill Street to Forches, then behind Okefield and up George Hill to Barnstaple Cross, and then on to Copplestone and Bow. The road to Barnstaple took a very different route to the one it does at the time of writing, branching off to Newbuildings (probably at Forches Cross) and thence to Morchard Bishop before joining the present A377 somewhere near Lapford. The main roads therefore did not go through the centre of the town.

The old line of the road between Crediton and Exeter is rather unclear. Col Montague tells us that 'the oldest road... branched off from the present road not far from Downes Mill, went along the Creedy valley to Commonmarsh Lane and thus to East Street.' It certainly seems that this is a more direct route than the present one. This route must have fallen out of use many centuries ago as the main road must have passed by the White Hart which has been the main coach-house in the East Town since the early-seventeenth century and possibly even earlier. Some historians talk of the main access to the town being over Fordton Bridge and up through Four Mills Lane, but with the other road being so direct it seems unlikely that this route was any more than a lane connecting the town with villages on the other side of the River Yeo.

The nineteenth century saw improvements to the road system which resulted in the roads to both Barnstaple and Okehampton being re-routed to run through the centre of the town. At the time this was seen as a great improvement as the resulting passing traffic brought greater trade to the town and speeded up access from the surrounding villages.

The twentieth century brought the greatest revolution in transport with the ever-growing popularity of the internal combustion engine. The arrival of the railway in 1851 may have opened travel up to many people, but the introduction of omnibus services and the charabanc took this a step further.

Mr Milton started a town service in the early 1920s between St Lawrence Green and the railway station, the buses timed to meet the trains. This service ran from Monday to Saturday. During the general strike of 1926 he started a service between Crediton and Exeter which included an early-morning bus to ferry workers to Willey's engineering works in St Thomas. In 1931 the Ministry of Transport altered the bus timetable, which proved unpopular with the towns-people, and some 200 patrons signed a petition of protest which was supported by the Urban District Council. The protest was successful and the hourly service to the city was restored. Milton continued to operate this service, in competition with Devon

*A group of young admirers examining the latest technology – Mr Dicker's new tricycle, c.1880. (CAHMS)*

General, until the Second World War when it was initially taken over by Greenslade's and then by the nationalised Exeter City Bus Company and Devon General. Mr Milton's fares were cheaper than his competitors, and a condition of the sale was that prices were not increased. It was not until the 1960s that this proviso was lifted, so for a number of years travellers between Crediton and Exeter enjoyed cheaper fares than those in the rest of the county.

Milton's bus company also ran excursions to the seaside and other places of interest and entertainment, as well as the 'mystery' trip. The works, club or pub outing was an annual event to be looked forward to as a highlight of the year. These trips seem to have gone out of fashion in recent years, but they survived long into the period when most homes had a car of their own.

Way & Sons were one of the main suppliers of these services in the postwar years. Their coaches were garaged at the bottom of Market Street where the fire station and the council car park are sited in 2004. Their main rivals were the Bow Belle company which operated initially from North Tawton, but in the early 1970s it moved into Crediton after taking over John Way's company. Bow Belle continued to operate until the end of the twentieth century, by which time the nature of its operations had changed, with the emphasis moving to long-distance and international travel.

In the early-twenty-first century the vast majority of journeys are by private car and volumes of traffic have increased significantly, especially in the later years of the twentieth century. Some of the pictures of the High Street, taken not many years ago, indicate how rapidly the situation has changed. For example, issues of the *Crediton Country Courier* from the late 1970s contain a debate on the need for yellow lines in the town, with some correspondents arguing that the number of vehicles did not warrant it.

Our predecessors would surely have thanked the far-sighted people who were responsible for improving the prosperity of this market town by improving the road system. However, there are many today, blighted by the volume of traffic in the town, who might wish that these improvements had never been carried out.

The question of a bypass for Crediton is one that causes great debate and argument in 2004, and no doubt will for years to come. This is not the place to contribute to that argument on one side or the other, but surely if those improvements of previous centuries had not been carried out then a resolution of the issue would have been forced upon the authorities some years ago.

*A Garford bus, as used by Milton's on the Crediton to Exeter service in the 1920s. (CAHMS)*

*Milton's staff in front of their 1929 Chevrolet coach with a third axle added. (CAHMS)*

*Coaches belonging to John Way and Bow Belle, c.1960. (CAHMS)*

*Councillor Charles Hawkins handing the keys of a new Volvo B10M to William Phillips, owner of Bow Belle,*
*with his sons Roger and Keith looking on, 1984.  (CAHMS)*

# The Crediton Canal

The construction of a canal between Exeter and Crediton, and possibly on to North Devon, was not one of the more successful ventures of the early-nineteenth century. On 3 October 1793 the *Exeter Flying Post* published an announcement of a public meeting at the Ship Hotel, Crediton, which would give details of progress towards funding the 'Public Devonshire Canal'. Some 15 years later it was announced that a canal from the Quay at Exeter via Cowley Bridge through the parish of Newton St Cyres, terminating at Four Mills, was complete as far as Exwick. However, there were no great hopes of it ever being completed, which, of course, it never was, but evidence of excavations near the station at Newton St Cyres have been found, which could well have been a 'cut' for this canal.

# The Railway

The railway arrived at Crediton on 2 May 1851, coincident with the opening of the Great Exhibition in London. The event was met with great celebrations in the town. The station was bedecked with bunting and the road as far as the White Hart was lined with an avenue of hundreds of trees.

The first train from Exeter was five carriages in length, but there were so many people that wanted to make the journey that, according to the *Western Times*, the train 'could not accommodate a third of the intended visitors.' A second train of nine carriages started ½ hour later, but apparently there were still many left behind.

A celebration luncheon for the local gentry was held at the Market House. Sir Humphrey Ferguson Davie Bart proposed the toast to the Exeter & Crediton Railway Company, stating that he had:

*... no doubt that this railway would be one of the greatest possible advantages that could be conferred, not only on the town of Crediton and its immediate neighbourhood, but on the whole of North Devon.*

In reply Elias Ward said that Crediton had 'now taken its place on the great arterial communication of England.' The following day the poor of the town were given the remnants of the feast, along with 'plenty of beer and cider.'

The arrival of the railway in Crediton had been long awaited – indeed it should have happened some four years earlier – but due to a dispute between rival companies the opening was delayed. Work commenced on the line in 1845 and was completed in

just 18 months. The line was laid as a 'double-broad gauge', as used by Brunel for his Great Western Railway, but it lay idle for four years whilst the Bristol & Exeter Railway Company and the London & South Western argued over which gauge should be used. Later in 1862, when the London & South Western line reached Exeter, a third rail was laid to allow trains of either gauge to use the line.

The contract for the laying of the line was given to J.J. Thomas, but a local builder, William Berry, won the contract for the building of the station and the construction of a number of the bridges. The firm is known today as Berry & Vincent, and the 'day books for that period still survive'. The entry for 29 July 1846 reads 'Station – Self to Exeter. Signed Contracts.' On the 5 August: 'Station... Commenced this day.' Ten workers were sent to the site that morning. Although the work was carried out by local men, it is thought that the designs for the station building were possibly by Brunel.

Berry carried out a great deal of construction work on the line. There are lengthy descriptions of work at Codshead Bridge and of the construction of a station at Cowley Bridge where the branch line meets the main London to Penzance line.

There is a story that whilst the line was lying idle as a result of the dispute Mr Berry took his family on an outing along the weed-strewn line, by attaching a horse (or two) to a goods truck and travelling as far as Cowley by rail instead of road. If this tale is true, then the first 'rail' journey on the Crediton branch line was earlier than 1851!

In May 2001 celebrations to mark the 150th anniversary of the opening of the line were held in the station precincts. A steam train was due to travel

*Cutting the cake at the railway's 150th celebrations.* Left to right: *M. André Ruault (President Crediton Avranches Partenaire), M. Michel Bezin (First Deputy Mayor Avranches), Mr Henry Parker, Cllr Bob Edwards (Mayor of Crediton), Mrs Linda Rogers, Mrs Jenny Pitts, Mrs Ruth Redman.* (Crediton Country Courier)

*Steam engine 'Bodmin' at Crediton, 30 September 2000. (CAHMS)*

*'Bodmin' leaving Crediton for Okehampton. The carriages are in the old Southern Railway green livery.*

*(CAHMS)*

*Crediton Railway Station in the days of steam and the horse-drawn cab.*
*(CAHMS, VALENTINE SERIES)*

*A train from Waterloo arriving at Crediton. The train used to be split at Exeter Central Station, then both halves would come through Crediton. At Yeoford Junction one would go to Barnstaple and the other via Okehampton to Plymouth. (CAHMS)*

*'Cab, Sir'. Waiting for a fare at the station. The cabby is thought to be Bob Boxer. (MRS W. DAVEY)*

to Crediton from Hampshire and on arrival be renamed Crediton, but unfortunately the engine broke down and was unable to make the journey. However, the organisers were blessed with fine weather and there were many stalls, sideshows and entertainers (many in Victorian costume), and the day was a great success.

The arrival of the railway was one of the most significant events of the nineteenth century for the town of Crediton. It was greeted with great celebrations in the town and hailed as a great hope for a prosperous future. Many twentieth-century historians, notably the eminent Devon historian Professor W.G. Hoskins, saw the railway as bringing about the decline of small market towns such

as Crediton. Writing in the 1950s he argued that in Crediton's case 'though it gave temporary stimulus to some by providing much-needed employment for a few years', by bringing the larger markets of Exeter just 20 minutes journey away, the local market suffered. Although the Crediton market did survive for a further 100 years, it cannot be denied that the nature of the town has changed; with improved transport systems, including both road and railway, bringing Exeter within easy reach Crediton has become something of a dormitory town. Indeed, since the early years of the twentieth century it is thought that around one in five of our population make the daily journey to our larger neighbour to work.

# Chapter 13

# Crediton in Time of War

The two world wars of the twentieth century had a significant impact on Crediton, as they did on every town and village in the country.

The First World War claimed the lives of 137 men from Crediton and Crediton hamlets. The number of wounded is not recorded, but dealing with them was a major undertaking in the latter years of the war and the days that followed. Very little information remains about the Red Cross hospitals in Crediton other than a few photographs. These indicate that there were two, possibly three hospitals in the town. One was at Newcombes and another was behind the High Street on the Barnfield side, near the site of St Saviours Car Park. It is also possible that the workhouse, or temporary accommodation on that site, was also used. Although these photographs do not give us clear evidence of exactly where they were situated they do give some indication of the number of people that needed hospital or convalescent care in those days. The end of this war was met with great celebrations and a peace-day parade in July 1919, when most of the returning troops were back in Crediton.

The Second World War did not bring as many military casualties, nevertheless, there are 40 names carved on the war memorial. What is clear is the deep-seated support for the men who were fighting for their country. In 1944 a 'Salute the Soldier Week' was organised to raise money to equip the men of the Devonshire Regiment. Crediton had a group called the 'Home Service Guild' which was also known as the 'Crediton Welcome Home Fund'. This group organised dances and other social events throughout the war to provide gifts for the troops. In all they sent over 1,000 parcels, each valued at around 10s. (50p). These parcels contained cigarettes, writing paper and envelopes, a pencil, razor blades, a comb, boot polish, boot laces, shaving soap, a tooth brush, woollen clothing (socks and a scarf), and a stamped addressed envelope to be sent back to the collectors. On returning on leave each serviceman was given 5s.

(25p) and a pack of cigarettes, and a servicewoman was given the same amount of money, but a bar of chocolate instead of the cigarettes. Returning prisoners of war were given £5 each – there were 13 recipients. The story of one these men is told in the next chapter.

Crediton was fortunate to avoid any serious bombing in the war, as only one bomb is recorded as falling in the town. This is thought to have been a stray bomb unloaded by a German bomber on his way home from a raid on Plymouth. It fell in a field near the milk factory and caused some relatively minor damage to the Parish Church.

On 8 June 1946, having allowed a suitable period for the troops to return home, a service of thanksgiving was held at the Parish Church and Armistice Day that year was marked with a 'Festival of Remembrance and Thanksgiving' held at the Palace Cinema.

## Crediton War Memorial

The Crediton Town and Hamlets War Memorial was unveiled by Field Marshall Sir William Robertson Bart, on Wednesday 16 May 1923. The ceremony was also attended by the Bishop of Crediton and the Guard of Honour was provided by the Depot of the Devon Regiment.

The money to build the memorial was raised by public subscription. The largest single contributor was Captain S. Shotton who donated £70. In all over £640 was raised. It is an impressive construction which was designed by Frederick Bligh Bond. It was built of Posbury stone, with panels of Portland Stone inscribed with the names of the fallen. As far as can be ascertained Crediton's was the only war memorial designed by Bond.

The memorial was renovated at the end of the twentieth century, partly thanks to the late Professor Chris Brooks, who constructed a case for the building to be listed. This listing resulted in a grant from English Heritage towards the cost of these renovations.

*Some of the 300 Crediton men who volunteered in 1914, on their way to join the 6th Devons. Note that they are standing on the 'down' platform – they went to Barnstaple, not Exeter, to enlist.*

(CAHMS, PHOTO BERRY)

*Part of the main parade at the Peace Day celebrations, 19 July 1919. (MRS W. DAVEY, PHOTO BERRY)*

*'Entertaining the Wounded'. A tea party held at Newcombes on Rose Day, 1917.*
*(CAHMS, PHOTO BERRY)*

*Crediton VAD (Voluntary Aid Detachment) Hospital during the Second World War. It is thought to have been located in or near the former Liberal Club, now the Redvers Buller public house. (CAHMS, PHOTO BERRY)*

Considerable research has been carried out in an attempt to find out who built the memorial, but without success. Records of the two main building firms in the town in the 1920s, Dart & Francis and Berry & Vincent, give no mention of carrying out the work, and despite appeals in local newspapers nobody has been able to come up with firm information. It is very likely, however, that one or both of these firms did the work as it was common for contracts to be given to a local company.

One possibility raised is that Berry & Vincent did the stonework and Dart & Francis the timber work. However, a former Dart & Francis stonemason, now departed, is reported to have claimed that the quality of the stonework could only be that of Dart & Francis!

Further Portland Stone panels were added after the Second World War, and we do know that Dart & Francis carried out this work. The ceremony to unveil these panels was held on Remembrance Sunday, 7 November 1948. It took place following the annual wreath-laying ceremony and was carried out by Lt Gen. Sir Edward Schreiber KCB. Following the ceremony Lt Gen. Schreiber took the salute from a base located outside the Midland Bank in Union Road.

There are 137 names of Crediton people who fell in the First World War and 40 from the Second World War. There is one further name on the memorial, that of Derek Millard who was killed by a sniper in Aden in 1965. Fortunately no Crediton citizens were lost during the Falklands or either of the Gulf Wars.

*The Crediton War Memorial unveiling ceremony, 16 May 1923.*

(PLIMSOLE COLLECTION, PHOTO BERRY)

# Roll of Honour of Men of Crediton
## Lost in Twentieth-Century Wars
### 1914–18

| | | |
|---|---|---|
| E. Adams | A.J. Borne | W.J. Colwill |
| C. St. Lo Auber | W. Brealy | W.G. Conabeer |
| W. Backwell | W. Bubear | G. Cooper |
| E.J. Baker | W.G. Bubear | J. Courtnay |
| O.A. Bere | E.W. Burridge | G. Crossman |
| S.E. Bere | F. Burridge | W. Darch |
| W. Berry | F. Cann | H.W. Davie |
| L.W. Blatchford | W.H. Chamberlain | J. Delve |
| W.H. Blatchford | W. Charlton | W.S. Doddridge |
| P. Boddy | P.J. Coles | S. Dymond |
| G.T. Body | R. Coles | H.F. Edwardes |

J. Elston
S.G. Elston
C.H. Erscott
F.H. Erscott
C.J. Flood
H. Frost
T. Frost
J.R. Fursman
F. Gale
A.F. Gallin
G. German
E.W. Gillman
R.C. Gillman
S.A. Gillman
S.J. Glover
A. Goddard
W.J. Grant
B.C. Gribble
G.L. Gribble
W. Gush
W.J. Hallett
F. Harry
W.A. Hatch
J.G. Hawker
F. Hellier
R. Henderson
R.P. Hill
F.W. Hooper
G.A. Hooper
W. Ireland
S.P. Jeffries
C. Johns
L.A. Keen
J. Land
T. Lane

A.C. Lang
W. Leach
C. Lee
B.J. Long
F.H. Loosemore
H. Mallett
J. Mann
W. Mann
W.H. Mann
E.H. Mogridge
F.D. Montague
P.D. Montague
A. Mortimore
F.J. Narracott
H.C. Neiass
T. Nott
H.C. Organ
A. Parker
J. Parkyn
J. Parr
D. Passmore
A.J. Phillips
J.C. Phillips
A.G. Piney
H.H. Pitts
E.R. Pope
C.D. Porter
E.C. Purse
L.S. Purse
G.E. Ralph
T. Reed
J. Salter
G. Sanders
J.R. Sanders
R.A. Searle

C.L. Selley
F.G. Setter
J. Setter
S.J. Setter
P. Shapland
R. Shapland
P.J. Shipman
A. Skinner
J. Smith
H. Snell
J. Snell
G. Spear
A.C. Spearman
A. Sprague
J. Sprague
A.W. Staddon
L.H. Stemson
F. Stentiford
F. Stiff
B.G. Strong
F.J. Strong
I. Sutton
C.W. Symes
E.E. Tompkins
L.G. Tothill
E. Tremlett
F. Tremlett
S. Tucker
G. Turner
M. Turner
H.J. Venn
J. Warren
B.W. Way
A.T. White

## 1939–45

G. Arundell
C. Ball
W.F. Batters
G.A. Brueton
A.J. Cherry
C.G. Chudley
A.J. Cossins
R.A. Davey
J. Davidson
C. Discombe
S.L.H. Dummett
J.W. Dunn
J. Eakers
E.J. Edworthy

C. Farley
N.C. Fisher
S. Garnsworthy
A.C. Gillard
D. Hugo
P. Hugo
A.E. Harvey
E.J. Harvey
W.H. Jackman
E.H. Madge
F. Milton
G.V. Merrifield
E. Miller
B.J.C. Parker

C.G. Parker
V.M. Powlesland
H.M. Phillips
E.G. Radford
S. Rowe
T.A. Richardson
A.E. Saunders
A.J. Sprague
D.J. Vicary
J.W. Way
E.G. White
E. Williams

## Aden 1965

D. Millard

*Armistice Day in the 1950s. (CAHMS, PHOTO AUTHERS)*

## Upper Deck

Upper Deck is situated at the top of George Hill on the road between Forches and Barnstaple Cross, or as it used to be known, Higher Road.

The site started life purely as a covered reservoir to provide water for the town. Situated as it is at the top of a steep hill above the town, it was ideal to provide a good head of water for the whole area. The idea was first mooted in 1896 by the Urban District Council, but it took two years before the necessary permission was granted and the money to purchase the land was raised.

During the First World War a letter was received by the Council offering to place a number of seats on the site together with a flagstaff and a warning notice against damage to both. An anonymous donor offered to pay in full for the work and this was accepted by the Council. The purpose of the offer was to provide a recreation area for the people of the town when the war was over; and because of its position the site, until recently, allowed uninterrupted views over the Devon countryside as far as the edges of Dartmoor.

In August 1915 a letter was received by the Council from a Miss Adams inviting them to see the completed work and to declare the site officially open to the public.

On 19 July 1919 Peace Day was celebrated, and part of the festivities included the lighting of a number of navy flares from Upper Deck which could be seen from all around the town. Cecil Plimsole remembered the day and said that he recalled seeing pinpoints of light in the sky in the far distance where similar flares lit in other towns and villages were burning.

After the war, and for many generations to follow, Upper Deck became a popular place for courting couples to meet. Indeed one will often see a twinkle in the eye of Kirtonians of all ages when the name Upper Deck is mentioned.

In June 1979 Cecil Plimsole wrote in the *Crediton Country Courier* about his memories of Upper Deck.

[There] *were two wooden shelters, each with an inscribed plaque above the seat. As well, the larger outside seats had a piece of poetry painted on the top rail. These seats had moveable backs so that one could face either way. One of the verses came from Longfellow's 'A Psalm of Life' namely:*

*Lives of great men all remind us
We can make our lives sublime,
And, departing, leave behind us
Footprints on the sands of time.*

In the years of the early-twenty-first century the site has been allowed to fall into disrepair, but it is hoped that in the very near future funds can be raised to restore it to its former state.

*19 July 1919, Peace Day celebrations. VAD nurses parade in the High Street.*

(MRS W. DAVEY)

*Armistice Day, 1939. This must have been a particularly solemn occasion in view of the recently commenced hostilities. Note that there are not many young men on parade or in the crowd. (CAHMS)*

*A Land Army girl at work on a farm near Crediton during the Second World War. (CAHMS)*

# Chapter 14

◇

# Some Notable Kirtonians
# of Modern Times

## Les Ashplant

Les was born in Crediton on 12 November 1923 of local parents. His father died when he was just 12 years of age and he was required to go out to work part time for Burridge & Elston, delivering shoes, before he finished his schooling aged 14.

As a boy he had always had the ambition to be a pilot and when he reached the age of 16 he joined the Air Training Corps. He was working as a printer at Jackson's factory, but in an attempt to obtain the necessary qualifications to become a pilot he undertook evening classes at the Grammar School. By this time war had broken out and as soon as he reached his 18th birthday he went to the recruiting office in Market Street to volunteer. He passed his medical for the RAF and was given the badge of the RAF Volunteer Reserve to show his status and to indicate why he was not at the Front.

Les was unable to obtain a position as a pilot, but was asked to volunteer as a gunner. Despite the high risk of the job he did volunteer and soon found himself in a very 'posh' block of flats in London's West End, which had been taken over by the RAF as temporary barracks. He was then sent to the Isle of Man for a gunnery course where he came out top in his group. He remembers that there were a number of 'enemy' prisoners held on the island, many of German origin but, in particular, he recalls Oswald Moseley being held there.

From the Isle of Man he was sent to RAF Stradishall in Suffolk. He first flew with Wing Commander Max, a New Zealander, as his gunner, but was soon replaced by a friend of the Wing Commander. He was not unoccupied for long, as Roy Bennett, an Australian, invited him to join his crew. This was a real international crew with men from Canada and Sierra Leone as well as the Australian skipper, but they quickly built a really close relationship. However, on only their third mission together they were shot down on the way to Mannheim. Les believes that he owes his life to his pilot Roy Bennett who somehow kept the aircraft stable with both port engines out of action, thus allowing all on board to bale out safely.

On 18 November 1943, Les found himself in a ploughed field on a cold and frosty night, and set out to walk to Switzerland. Unfortunately he did not get very far. As dawn approached he found himself near a farmhouse and went to look for a barn, or somewhere similar, where he could sleep until it was dark again. However, the farmyard proved to be the site of a searchlight crew, and Les soon found himself with a rifle in his back and hearing a loud command, in German, to put his hands up. He was taken to the nearest railway station and put on a train which took him to Düsseldorf where he was placed in a prison cell. For some reason the local police took him on a tour of the vineyards of the Rhine and Moselle region; presumably to show off the German landscape. Next he was taken to Frankfurt where he was placed in a cell 6ft by 8ft, and subjected to interrogation. During this interrogation it became clear to Les that the Germans knew more than he did, and he was eventually 'released' to a prisoner-of-war camp.

It was a long journey to the camp (Stalag 4B), which was situated in the east on the far bank of the River Elbe. On arrival the prisoners were stripped off and given injections against disease. The diet was very poor with rations confined to potatoes and bread. It was only the Red Cross parcels that kept them alive. However, the Russians in the camp were in a much worse state because, as they did not recognise the Red Cross, they did not receive any parcels to supplement their diet. They would give concerts to the British in return for scraps of food. Many of the Russian prisoners died of malnutrition.

Les was in the camp for around 18 months. There were 240 prisoners in each hut, sleeping in bunks four high, the newest prisoners having to sleep at floor level. The regime was to parade at 6a.m. every day – one of his most lasting of memories was the extreme cold in winter months. If and when the inmates had the strength they would play football.

*Les Ashplant with his RAF colleagues in 1943.  Left to right: Hal Gourlie (Canadian), Les Milnethorpe, Les Ashplant, Ray Bennett (pilot, Australian), Frank Matthews, Bill Hutchings, Jonny Smythe MBE (Sierra Leone).  (Les Ashplant)*

There was also a library, but they were often too cold or tired to be able to concentrate sufficiently to read for any length of time.

There were escape plans, one in particular where a tunnel was built under the library which went out into a field of rye just beyond the perimeter wire. Unfortunately, about two days before the planned escape, the farmer decided to cut the rye, and his tractor collapsed the roof of the tunnel and fell into the hole.

Another Kirtonian, George Matten (father of Alan), was also in the camp. He used to cut the prisoners' hair for the price of two cigarettes.

Les recalls that they were fairly well treated by the Germans, who had very little more food to eat than the prisoners did. However, towards the end of the war the Germans deserted the camp, a couple of days before the Russians arrived. They were right to be afraid as the Russians showed no respect for their enemies; men women or children.

Freedom did not come immediately after the war. The prisoners were now in the hands of the Russians and there was a real fear that they would be sent to work in Siberia. They were first sent in an east-wardly direction to Risa, where they remained for three weeks. Whilst billeted there they saw the true state of the ordinary German citizens in the east; they were in as bad or even worse a condition than many of the Russian prisoners. Les remembers that he used to break into trains to obtain food and, despite having been their prisoner for 18 months, he gave some of this food to the local Germans.

Eventually the Americans arrived and the prisoners were ordered to quickly get into the trucks and were driven across the one remaining bridge over the River Elbe and on to Leipzig. Here they were treated like lords by the Americans. Next it was to Halle airport and a flight back to Brussels where they were picked up by the RAF.

On arrival back on British soil the men stayed at Cosford for a couple of days to be re-kitted. Les then came back to Barnfield and a long leave. However, Les did not think that his war was over because he expected to return to duty against the Japanese. Fortunately they surrendered before his leave was over.

He married his wife Margaret in 1947 and they had two children, Elaine and Nigel. He had met Margaret before the war, but they decided to go their separate ways for the duration. Margaret served with the WAAF as a wireless operator, and at the end of the war she was posted to Cornwall and decided to search Les out. She invited him to visit her in Cornwall, and within two years they were married.

After the war Les went back to Jackson's, but he was not given his old job in the printing office. He was approached by Bertram Authers to work for him in his photography business located behind the cinema. He worked for Bert until he died and even carried on after Bert's successor Derek Folland retired. Many people will remember Les in this capacity, for he was a photographer in the town from 1945 until around 1990 when he retired. During this time anyone who got married in the town would probably have had their wedding photographs taken by Les.

## Mary Blamey

Although Mary was born in Surrey she is of true Kirton stock. Her maternal grandfather was William Gillard who was foreman over the female workers in the machine room at Gimblett's Economic Shoe Works in the High Street. Her paternal grandfather, John Snow, was a carpenter with Dart & Francis and travelled all over England and Scotland with that firm. Her father, Fred, spent 20 years in the London area working for the railway, but in 1932 he was appointed as the stationmaster at Camelford in Cornwall and it was there that Mary met and married her husband, Ned. He spent the war years in the RAF, and on his return discovered that Mary and her parents had moved to Crediton. The couple therefore decided to make Crediton their home.

They built their first house in 1948, which was Mary's first contact with the Council, when there was an argument about the site of their garage and the building of an electricity station beside the house. She had always been interested in politics but it was not until Mark Bonham Carter won the 1958 by-election that she took an active part (having produced three daughters by then). After this she started to work for the Liberal party in an administrative capacity, first as secretary of the area committee and later as treasurer of the Torrington Division.

She was invited to stand as a Liberal candidate for the Crediton Urban District Council alongside Malcolm Perkins. Malcolm topped the poll and Mary, much to her surprise, was also elected. In 1971 she became the UDC's one and only woman chairman.

In 1973 she won the Devon County Council seat for Crediton. This was shortly after the county had been reorganised to include both Plymouth and Torbay (until then independent). Representatives of these areas were reluctant county councillors, and for a time the atmosphere in the Council Chamber was somewhat difficult. She lost her DCC seat in 1977. The main events in Devon during her four years on

*Mary Blamey, pictured in 1983.*

(CREDITON COUNTRY COURIER)

the Council were the designing and building of Roadford Reservoir and the proposed upgrading of the A30 through the county.

In 1975 the UDC was scrapped and Crediton became part of Tiverton District Council (soon to be properly named Mid Devon). However, Alan Swann, who was a sitting councillor and was leaving the area, persuaded her to stand in the by-election for his seat. On reorganisation she also became a town councillor and served on that Council until the age of 70 when she decided to give up politics. She served as chairman on four occasions, one of which was the year of the Queen's silver jubilee, 1977.

Whilst on the DCC she had been a member of the Social Services Committee, which led to a personal interest in Age Concern Devon. She later served for five years as chairman of the Devon branch. Mary feels that her greatest achievement was in starting the Crediton branch of this organisation. In 2004 she is proud to say that Age Concern in Crediton has its own premises in Deep Lane and a charity shop in the High Street.

In retirement Mary was instrumental in forming the Crediton Area History and Museum Society in 1984, and served as both secretary and treasurer for many years.

# Dr Margaret Jackson (1898–1987)

Dr Jackson was a controversial figure in the field of family planning in the middle years of the twentieth century. Her work on contraception and 'artificial insemination' was many years ahead of its time and often ahead of public opinion. Indeed, in 1999 there was controversy in the national media over the outcome of her work.

She was born and brought up in the South East. At the end of the First World War she was admitted as a student at the Medical School of University College London. In those days it was still most unusual for a woman to be trained at such a prestigious establishment. During the time she was at the college she met and married Lawrence Jackson, who was also a medical student there. In 1926, soon after her husband qualified, he moved to Crediton as a general practitioner and she joined him in the town. Dr Lawrence Jackson is fondly remembered in the town, serving as a GP in the High Street (now Chiddenbrooke) practice for around 30 years.

In those days operations were often carried out in the patient's home, or in the Jacksons' case at Kenwyn Nursing Home. They were both strong supporters of Kenwyn, to the point that when the home was in danger of closing in the 1950s they bought it themselves in an attempt to keep it open.

Dr Margaret opened her first family-planning clinic in Sidwell Street in Exeter in 1930. This is believed to have been the first such clinic in the South of England. Prior to this time it was not uncommon for women to have more than 10 pregnancies and the purpose of the clinic was to help couples plan their families and the number of children they produced. In 1934 Devon was cited as the best-provided county in the whole country for family-planning services, and it is down to Dr Margaret Jackson that this was achieved. In later years she was involved with the launch of the contraceptive pill, speaking in favour of the project at both medical conferences and public meetings.

However, her specialist area was in helping sub-fertile and infertile couples. Her first 'artificial insemination' baby was born in the mid-1930s. At that time work in this field was so controversial that it had to be carried out in the utmost secrecy, but as her career progressed she gained an international reputation, and her work is seen as instrumental in the development of the 'test tube' and IVF methods of fertilisation.

The Sidwell Street Clinic has been moved several times since the 1930s and at the time of writing is situated in Barnfield Hill, Exeter. It still gives advice on family planning and fertility problems and is now called the Margaret Jackson Centre, in honour of its founder's work.

However, this work is not seen in such a positive light by all. Because of the need for secrecy in the early days, records of the 'fathers' to the artificial-insemination children were not kept in the public domain, and when Dr Jackson died in 1987 many of her personal records were destroyed. In the summer of 1999 Channel 4 made a documentary featuring some of these children who had been unsuccessfully searching for their 'natural' fathers. Their resentment towards Dr Jackson was clear. Controversy, therefore, has not only followed her during her lifetime, but to the grave as well.

## Arthur Richardson MBE
## Musical Instrument Maker
## 1880–1965

Arthur Richardson lived much of his life in a small cottage off Park Street near Huniver's Place, and worked in a shed at the bottom of his garden. Both the cottage and shed have been demolished, but the shed used to stand on what, at the time of writing, is a grassy triangle above the level of the road.

Arthur was born in a Derbyshire village in 1880. He loved music from an early age and played in the village band. At 14 he left school and was apprenticed to a pattern-maker in a foundry in Leeds, but his heart was not in his work. He soon realised he had a talent for wood carving and set his mind to becoming an expert in that field.

Soon after the First World War he came to Crediton and started making musical instruments. He entered one of his first violins into a music competition and it won first prize. The reputation he earned from this allowed him to sell some of his instruments and raise enough capital to start his own business.

Some years later he met Lionel Tertis, a world-famous viola player, at a concert in Bideford. Tertis was not satisfied with the results that he was getting from his instrument and talked over with Richardson some revolutionary ideas. In the past the viola had been an instrument that was played between the knees, as the cello still is. Tertis thought it could be made a little smaller, without losing tone or quality,

so that it could be played under the chin, similar to a violin. After years of work the new model was perfected and since then the name of Richardson has become world famous. His instruments have been played by musicians in many of the greatest orchestras of the world. It is claimed that in 1951 he attended a concert at the Wigmore Hall where seven of the violas had been made by him. More than 100 Richardson-Tertis violas were made.

Richardson would spend hours, sometimes days, making the minute modifications necessary to achieve the 'perfect' tone; changes that only a master of the instrument would notice. Throughout his life he made over 500 stringed instruments. Often, in fine weather, you could see instruments hung out to dry in his little shed at the bottom of the garden.

He has been honoured with a blue plaque for his contribution to music. As his cottage and workshop are gone the plaque has been erected in Newcombes Meadow close to the bowling-green, where he enjoyed his other passion in life.

## Arthur Henry King Robinson

Arthur King Robinson is a member of a family that has lived in Crediton continuously since 1856. He was born on 16 May 1914 at Esquimalt, Victoria, in British Columbia. His mother was Doris Symes, third daughter of William Henry Symes. She was born at the Manor House, Parliament Street, Crediton. His father was Henry King Robinson of the Indian Forestry Service, seconded to British Columbia for the formation of that Government Forestry Department, having been commissioned in the Canadian Royal Artillery. His mother, who was one of the first members of the Chartered Society for Massage and Medical Gymnastics (today's physiotherapists), brought her son back to England when her husband's unit came to France early in the First World War. After the war the family returned to Victoria, British Colombia until 1921 when his father returned to the Indian Forestry Service and his mother brought their son and daughter to Crediton, the Symes family home town.

Before spending two years when aged eight to ten in the preparatory department of the High School, Arthur had private tuition by a Miss Martin and by Miss Bradbury of Hayward's School infants' department. From the age of ten to 13 he was a pupil at Crediton Grammar School, the first two years in the class of Mr Edmund Tompkins who had previously been the headmaster at Dunn's School (which had been started by William Dunn during the reign of George IV). At the age of 13 Arthur attended Blundell's School, Tiverton as a boarder.

At the age of 18 he was commissioned in the 4th Battalion Devon Regiment (Territorial Army) and recruited a platoon who drilled in the hut in Charlotte Street and for whom the 600-yard rifle-range at Aller Farm, West Sandford, was reopened after the last previous use in 1919.

He was then articled to John Symes, the solicitor practising from the east end of the Manor House. He qualified as a solicitor in November 1936 and joined his uncle in February 1937 when he opened a branch office in Budleigh Salterton.

In 1938, with war imminent, the Territorial Army was doubled in size. The 4th Battalion district was divided in two by the creation of the 8th Bn. Arthur was made the Company Commander of the Exmouth, Budleigh Salterton and Sidmouth Company of the 8th Bn. The 43rd Division of the TA, of which the 8th Devons formed a part, were concentrated in Devon, the 8th Bn at Yelverton, during the winter of 1939/40. In early May 1940 the Division was moved to Sevenoaks in Kent where Arthur was made Camp Commandant at Division HQ. During that summer the Division was moved to Crowborough and, later, Hawkhurst until after the end of the Air Force Battle of Britain in September 1940. The Division was then moved to Yorkshire.

Arthur then volunteered to join the West Country Division unit of the newly formed Reconnaissance Corps and was stationed in Spalding, Lincolnshire before being posted to India where, after acclimatisation, he was posted to the 9th Bn Royal Sussex Bn, then training near Poonah. They embarked at Calcutta to defend the Arakan – now the southern end of Bangladesh. The battalion took part in action there helping to prevent the Japanese from moving towards India. After the monsoon period a three-battalion Infantry Brigade moved to the north end of Assam (North East India) and were then flown into the north end of Burma where they came under American command as part of a plan to reopen the roads between India, Burma and China, moving southwards beside and across the River Irriwady. During that period the 9th Royal Sussex was in several actions, for one of which, Pinwee, the battalion was awarded a battle honour. Arthur was ranked Major at this time and commanded a company.

In February 1945 Arthur was granted compassionate leave to return to England following the death of his uncle John Symes, the only solicitor in the practice at Crediton or Budleigh Salterton. On return to Crediton he was appointed clerk to the Crediton bodies of which his uncle John Symes had been clerk. These were the Crediton Urban District Council, the Crediton Church Governors, the Crediton United Charities, the Hayward's Charity, the Governors of Crediton Grammar School and the Governors of Crediton High School for Girls. In 1947 he initiated the founding of the Crediton Chamber of Commerce and the formation of the Newcombes Housing Association. He was a founder member of the postwar League of Friends of Crediton Hospital and the Crediton Area History and Museum Society.

In 1951 he married Cynthia Huxley of Abergavenny, Monmouthshire, a member of the Huxley family of science fame. They have one adopted daughter, Sarah, who was born in Kenwyn Nursing Home and at the time of writing is a senior matron at Blundell's School, Tiverton.

In 2004 Arthur is a committee member of

*Arthur King Robinson in conversation with Dr Fisher, Archbishop of Canterbury, at the St Boniface celebrations of 1954. (CAHMS, PHOTO AUTHERS)*

*The last appeal.  Gifty Steer is pictured at Crediton Carnival.  (PHOTO AUTHERS)*

Newcombes (Crediton) Housing Association, Crediton Area History and Museum Society, and joint Hon. Secretary of the Friends of Crediton Hospital. He is also one of the 12 governors of Crediton Church.

## Frederick 'Gifty' Steer

During his lifetime there must have been hardly a single resident of the town who did not know or had at least heard of Gifty Steer.  He gave 57 years' service to rugby, both as a player and an administrator, and he was a fire-fighter for many years and made the 'last appeal' at the carnival his own.  He earned the nickname Gifty in his school-days, as whenever he was asked to do anything he would always reply that he would do it in a 'jiffy'.  The name became so well established that there are probably many people who knew him as 'Gifty' and never knew his real name.

He played his first game of rugby for Crediton at the beginning of the 1930/31 season.  Initially he was a wing-forward, but soon converted to full-back.  As with many players of this era the war interrupted a playing career which came to an end in 1946. Nevertheless, his association with the club continued as an administrator.  He was chairman between 1953 and 1971, the period of the club's greatest growth. During this time in the chair, Crediton RFC progressed from using the Oatsheaf as its changing-rooms, through the purchase of the former fire station in Exhibition Road, to the construction and development of the present clubhouse.  He was president of the club from 1971 to 1977 when he was made a life member.  In 1980 he was awarded the *Express and Echo* 'Services to Sport Award'.  On his death in 1984 Jack Hayes wrote in tribute 'no man is indispensable, but some are irreplaceable.'

During the Second World War he was a driver in the Service Corps, reaching the rank of Staff Sergeant. His first posting was to North Africa in 1942 and he was among the first to land at Salerno in Italy. Following the end of hostilities he was posted for a short period to Graz in Austria with the Army of Occupation.  On his return to Crediton he resumed his duties as a volunteer fire-fighter and later became the station's Chief Officer.

Most Crediton people will remember Gifty as a great character and for the 'last appeal' at the carnival; almost shouting himself hoarse, he would cajole the last few pennies out of the watching crowds in the High Street.

After his death in 1984 a memorial fund was set up to raise money for the Crediton Hospital.  In six years £15,000 was raised, £10,000 going towards an extension which has been named after him in his honour.  The remainder was also donated to the hospital.

*A very old photo. The gentleman in the cab is thought to be Dr Hugo. (CAHMS, PHOTO HECTOR)*

*The annual outing of Elston's shoe factory staff, c.1904. The driver of the front cab is Albert Borne and the other driver is Mr Frost. The man holding the horse of the front cab is Walter Radford who worked at the Ship Hotel stables. (MRS W. DAVEY)*

# Bibliography

## BOOKS

Bridget Cherry and Nikolas Pevsner, *The Buildings of England: Devon.*  Penguin Books, London, 1989.
W.G. Hoskins, *Devon.*  Collins, London, 1954.
Paul Harris, *Crediton Rugby: The First 125 Years.*  Paul Harris, Crediton, 2003.
Kenneth Hudson, *Towards Precision Shoemaking.*  David & Charles, Newton Abbot, 1968.
Charles Luxton, 'The Tun by the Creedy', in the *Transactions of the Devonshire Association for the Advancement of Science, Literature and Art, 1955, Vol.lxxxvii*, pp33 to 38.
William Pope, *Glimpses of the Past in and Around Crediton.*  Gregory and Son, Tiverton, 1927.
Timothy Reuter (Ed), *The Greatest Englishman: Essays on St Boniface and the Church at Crediton.*  Paternoster Press, Exeter, 1980.
Major T.W. Venn, *Crediton als Critton als Kirton and Hereabouts.*
Colin White, *The History of the Congregational Church in Crediton.*  Colin White, Crediton, 2003.

## PAMPHLETS

Hilary Davies, *Catholics in Crediton: A Brief History.*
Sidney Dixon, *Crediton Methodist Church: Centenary 1892 – 1992.*  Phillips & Co., Crediton, 1991.
Babs Stutchbury, *Of Creedy.*  Marion Aubry, 1995.

# Subscribers

Robin E. Abrahams, Crediton, Devon
David and Elizabeth Adams, Crediton, Devon
Christopher James Allard, Crediton, Devon
A. Alsopp, Sandford, Devon
Eric J. Anning
Mrs Maureen Archard (née Bater), Lapford, Crediton, Devon
Arthur and Helen Arscott
L.C. Ashplant
Brian Avery, Ludgershall, Wiltshire
Margaret Avery, Crediton, Devon
Michael (Tich) Avery, Exeter
Belinda Aylmer, The Hays, Ramsden, Oxford
Keith and Sue Barker, Crediton
Donna Batters, Northampton
Liz Bayley, Crediton, Devon
Glenn Bearne, Knowle, Crediton
Roger Bellamy, Crediton, Devon
Sidney Bicknell, Chorley, Lancashire
Dr Angela Blaen, Neopardy, Crediton
Mr Leslie Blake, Crediton
Mrs Mary Blamey, Crediton, Devon
Courtney J. Bond, Crediton, Devon
Katie L. Bond, Crediton, Devon
W. Richard Borne, Crediton, Devon
The Reverend David Boundy, Topsham
J. Bragg, Crediton, Devon
Kathleen J. Brashaw, Colebrooke
Lynne Brimilcombe, Copplestone
Frank R. Bristow, Trenavin, Crediton
Susan Brown, Crediton, Devon

Arthur C.W. Burge, Crediton, Devon
Lesley S.W. Burridge
K.J. Burrow, Bucks Cross, Devon
Sir Neil Butterfield
Ann Cann, Crediton
Irene Carpenter, Crediton
F.M. Champion, Crediton
Joan E. Charters, Crediton, Devon
Mr I.W. Chudley, Crediton, Devon
Colin and Patricia Cole, Crediton, Devon
Miss Irene Adeline Coles, Crediton, Devon
Cliff and Janet Conibear, West Sandford, Near Crediton, Devon
Sandra D. Cooper, Crediton, Devon
Derek Courtney, Torrington, Devon
Roy Courtney, Crediton, Devon
Adele Cox, Crediton
John Cutland, Hookway, Crediton
Eileen and Len Darling, Shobrooke
Janet and George Davey, Crediton
Eve Dennis, Shobrooke
Tony and Jeanne Dennis, Crediton
Gordon Dockings, Morchard Bishop
Colin and Ann Eakers, Crediton
Roy and Gill Edwards, Crediton, Devon
Mr Raymond A. Elliott, Cheriton Fitzpaine, Devon
D. and P. Ellis, Morchard Bishop
Albert E. Elston, Crediton, Devon
Joan Elston, Crediton, Devon
Anthony J. Elston, Crediton, Devon
John H. Facey, Crediton, Devon

Paul Fallon, Crediton
Dr Michael J. Fennessy, Crediton, Devon
Revd Anthony Freeman, Newton St Cyres
Mike and Sylvia Fry, Crediton
Courtney Garnsworthy, Crediton, Devon
Douglas J. Garnsworthy
Nan and John Gaskell, Crediton, Devon
Gary Grant, Crediton, Devon
Ivan Grant, Crediton, Devon
Ryan Grant, Crediton, Devon
I.G. and J.M. Grinney, Crediton, Devon
Jon and Anne Grubb, Crediton, Devon
Diane Hammett
Valerie M. Hann, Colebrooke, Crediton
Hilary Harris, Crediton, Devon
Joyce Harris, Crediton, Devon
Kevin Harvey, Crediton, Devon
Mr F. Heale, Sandford, Nr Crediton, Devon
Kenneth Hext, Crediton
A.J. Hill, Crediton, Devon
Mr William Hole, Crediton
Mr Tony D. Holloway, Tiverton, Devon
Derek, Ceredwin and Matthew Hooper, North Island, New Zealand/formerly Crediton, Devon
David Hubber, Crediton, Devon
Allan and Carol Isaac
Mr B.C. Jarvis, Knowle, Crediton, Devon
Doreen Jones, Horsford, Norwich
J.E. Jones
Norma Jones
Molly Kelly, Fordton, Crediton (1940)
Dave and Shirley King, Pennicott, Shobrooke
R. Langhorne
M.J. and W. Lankester, Crediton
R.G. and V.E. Lankester, Budleigh Salterton
Mr S. Lee, High Street, Crediton, Devon
C.J. and O.J. Leyman, Crediton, Devon
F.J. Luxmore, Rensey Farm, Lapford
K. Luxton, Crediton
Ann and Andrew Macbeth, Crediton, Devon
Mary Mason, Crediton, Devon
Katrina May, Crediton, Devon
Christine Moore, Crediton
Mr W.J. Moore, late of Hookway, Crediton
O.W. Gillian Morris, Lapford, Devon

Keith Mortimer, Searle Street, Crediton
D.J. Moss, D.Phil. (Oxon), Prof. Emeritus, Crediton, Devon
Mr R.P. Newlands, Creedy Park, Devon
Dr Bruce E. Newling, New Brunswick, USA
Elaine X. Nicholls, Dartford, Kent
Julie North, Lapford, Devon
Mary North, Morchard Bishop
Betty Nunn (née Lewis), Crediton
Mary Nunn, Cheriton Fitzpaine
Mr and Mrs Ofield, Crediton, Devon
Jenny and Rodney Opie, Feilding, New Zealand
George J. Palin, Crediton, Devon
Mrs Ellen Palmer, Crediton
Henry and Susan Parker, Downes, Crediton, Devon
Major P.H. Parker, The Hays, Ramsden, Oxford
Douglas Penny, Crediton
Linda Penny, Crediton, Devon
Paul Penny, Kingsteignton, South Devon
Mrs Maureen Penrose, Postmaster
Michael Pentreath, Exeter
Angela C.R. Perkins, Sandford, Devon
Mrs A. Perren, Bourne
Keith Phillips, Crediton
W.A. Pitts, Crediton, Devon
Roy and Shelagh Pollard, Crediton, Devon
Mr and Mrs L.A. Pope, Crediton, Devon
N.A. Powlesland, Crediton
David R. Price, Heavitree, Exeter
Bessie A. Pugsley, North Street, Crediton
Alan G. Quick, Crediton, Devon
Marian and Bill Quick, Loosebeare Manor
Jean M. Roach, Crediton, Devon
N.M. Roach
Mr A.H. King Robinson, Crediton, Devon
Wendy L. Rowe, Crediton, Devon
Diane Rowland, Sidcup, Kent
M. Sandercock, Crediton, Devon
Mr Michael R. Sanders, Crediton, Devon
Brenda Savage, Crediton, Devon
Wendy and Derek Searle
Alan D. Sharpe, Crediton, Devon
Charles Sheldrick, Cheriton Fitzpaine
Dr J.M. Shields, North Tawton, Devon
Ethel (Molly) Smith, Crediton, Devon
Mrs P. Smith, Crediton, Devon

Tony Snell, Crediton, Devon
Lyn Squire, Crediton
Anna M. Steele, Crediton, Devon
Mrs A. Steer
Ronald Stevens, Crediton, Devon
Trevor K. Stoneman
Babs Stutchbury (Delve)
Symonds Estate Agents, High Street, Crediton
June and Bill Taylor, Crediton
Don Teague, Crediton, Devon
Judith and David Thistlewood, Exeter
Brian and Mary Threlfall
Jeanette Titt, Crediton, Devon
Beryl Tregale, Crediton, Devon
P.J. Tregale, Crediton, Devon

Mr and Mrs G.W. Tregale, Crediton, Devon
Roger Trewhella and Adela Booth, Higher Moorlake
Sandra M. Tucker, Crediton, Devon
Fred Tuckett, Crediton, Devon
Mrs Lisa Turner, Crediton
John Twitchin, Crediton, Devon
Albert J. Vodden, Crediton, Devon
John F.W. Walling, Newton Abbot, Devon
Colin White, Crediton, Devon
Revd Michael and Mrs Ann Williams, Crediton
Hugh, Evelyn and George Willman, Crediton, Devon
Margaret Wollacott, Crediton
Mrs M. Wollacott, Crediton

*In order to include as many historical photographs as possible in this volume, a printed index is not included. However, the Devon titles in the Community History Series are indexed by Genuki.*

*For further information and indexes to various volumes in the series, please visit: http://www.cs.ncl.ac.uk/genuki/DEV/indexingproject.html*